I0020574

Logical Data Modeling

An Introduction to the
Entity-Relationship Model

Logical Data Modeling

An Introduction to the Entity-Relationship Model

George Tillmann

Stockbridge Press

Logical Data Modeling
An Introduction to the Entity-Relationship Model

Copyright © 2021 George Tillmann
All rights reserved.

ISBN: (paperback) 978-1-7338699-3-5
Library of Congress Control Number: 2021911605

This work is subject to copyright. All rights are reserved by the publisher (Stockbridge Press, Colts Neck, NJ), whether the whole or part of the material is concerned, specifically the rights of translation, reprinting, reuse of illustrations, recitation, broadcasting, reproduction on microfilms or in any other physical way, and transmission or information storage and retrieval, electronic adaptation, computer software, or by similar or dissimilar methodology now known or hereafter developed.

Trademarked names, logos, and images may appear in this book. Rather than use a trademark symbol with every occurrence of a trademarked name, logo, or image we use the names, logos, and images only in an editorial fashion and to the benefit of the trademark owner, with no intention of infringement of the trademark.

The use in this publication of trade names, trademarks, service marks, and similar terms, even if they are not identified as such, is not to be taken as an expression of opinion as to whether or not they are subject to proprietary rights.

Limit of Liability/Disclaimer of Warranty: While the publisher and author have used their best efforts in preparing this book, they make no representations or warranties with respect to the accuracy or completeness of the contents of this book and specifically disclaim any implied warranties of merchant ability or fitness for a particular purpose. No warranty may be created or extended by sales representatives or written sales materials. The advice and strategies contained herein may not be suitable for your situation. You should consult with a professional where appropriate. Neither the publisher nor author shall be liable for any loss of profit or any other commercial damages, including but not limited to special, incidental, consequential, or other damages.

Published by Stockbridge Press

For

Catherine, Gloria, Teresa, Carolyn, and Eva Marie

We are indebted to women, first for life itself, and then for making it worth having.
~ Adolfo Bioy Casares

Contents

Preface

It is not the data we want but the essence of the data.
~ John Cheever

Data is a precious thing and will last longer than the systems themselves.
~ Tim Berners-Lee

A database consultant for a mainframe computer company was visiting a customer site for a 2-day meeting. During lunch on the first day, she visited the database team. They were struggling with a performance problem. Their most important nightly job took more than 3 hours to run, putting time pressure on the entire night's production run. She looked at their database design and in less than 20 minutes recommended a few changes. She then went back to her meeting. The client database team tested her changes in their test environment, received approval to implement the changes, and had them in production by that evening. The next morning, before her second day meeting began, she received a note saying the critical production application had completed its run in 35 minutes the night before. This true story underscores a key fact about database design. If a computer program contains an error, it will either produce inaccurate results or, most likely, not run at all. The same is true for a network configuration. However, databases are different.

A poor database design might work, even though its inefficiency means performance is terrible. It all comes down to the knowledge and skill of the database designers. Inadequately trained information management staff produce substandard database designs. This common problem is often masked because the poor design works to some extent. Deficient database designs support critical applications all over the world—with everything from application code, to networks, to hardware blamed for their poor performance.

In addition, managing information has become increasingly complex in the last few decades. An astronomical increase in the kinds of data that organizations want to store, the volume of that data, and how organizations want to use it is straining systems development staff. While sloppy design might have gone unnoticed a few years ago, it has now become a business critical success factor.

Organizations are necessarily turning to more formal methods of designing databases. Any intelligent database design process begins with logical data modeling, and the best approach for modeling the data that an organization can use is the Entity-Relationship Model.

This beginner's book is for those interested in learning logical data modeling, but it is also suitable for the experienced data modeler who wants to expand his or her knowledge or learn some tips and tricks of the trade. This book is based on my more advanced book, *A Practical Guide to Logical Data Modeling (Second Edition)*, but contains additional information for those less familiar with the subject. Its three objectives are to:

- Present a platform-independent view of the basics of logical data modeling.

- Introduce a common set of principles to follow when data modeling, the adoption of which can go a long way toward reducing, if not eliminating, many common problems.

- Present a best practices approach—the lessons learned from dozens of experienced data modelers over decades of data modeling.

This book follows the Entity-Relationship Model created by Peter Chen in 1976 and includes a number of extensions introduced by various authors in subsequent years. There is no formal standard for logical data modeling; however, most of the world's logical data modelers have chosen to use the Entity-Relationship Model. Their decision is based on the model's simplicity of design, how accurately it can capture the true nature of an organization's data, its easy comprehension by business users and technical staff alike, and its independence from any database management or file system. Most data modeling software products support the Entity-Relationship Model.

Organization of the Book

Chapter 1 Models and Principles. Introduces the abstract model as a tool for understanding the real world. The chapter also presents the three logical design principles: Separation, Distinction, and Communication, which are "the 10 commandments" of logical design.

Chapter 2 Entities and Attributes. Introduces entities and attributes, two of the three basic logical data modeling objects.

Chapter 3 Relationships. Introduces the third logical data modeling object, relationships. Discussion includes the concepts of membership class, degree, domains, and valuations, among others.

Chapter 4 More About the Entity-Relationship Model. Expands the modeling basics to include: additional characteristics of entities, relationship constraints, attribute complexity and sources, among others.

Chapter 5 Building the Logical Data Model. Guides the data modeler through the steps to create an actual organization's logical data model and offers some best practices to follow for creating a successful model.

Chapter 6 Some Useful Techniques and Tips for Building a Logical Data Model. Introduces subject area diagrams, neighborhood diagrams, entity fragment diagrams, relationship bridges and stubs, the two logical data diagrams, clouds, enterprise models, and using data modeling and CASE tools.

Chapter 7 Physical Database Design. Presents a physical database design case to introduce what the users of the logical data model—the physical database designers (both the physical data modeler and the database schema designer)—need and what the logical data model must do to satisfy those needs.

Chapter 8 What About...? Answers some frequently asked questions about derived data, identifiers and keys, normalization, the multiple definitions of the term *logical data model*, many-to-many relationships, and data warehouses and big data.

Glossary. Defines the terms used in this book.

Chapter
1

Models and Principles

The sciences do not try to explain, they hardly even try to interpret,
they mainly make models. By a model is meant a mathematical construct which,
with the addition of certain verbal interpretations, describes observed phenomena.
~ John von Neumann

Those are my principles, and if you don't like them…well, I have others.
~ Groucho Marx (attributed)

Information technology (IT) builds computer-based systems and, according to numerous studies, IT is bad at it. For example, a McKinsey-Oxford University study of 5,400 IT projects found that, "on average, large IT projects run 45 percent over budget and 7 percent over time while delivering 56 percent less value than predicted."[1] Many projects hit the IT trifecta—late, over budget, and functionally poor. These results are, unfortunately, confirmed time and again, in study after study. Whatever IT is doing, it is not doing it right. At the same time, there are many promising remedies out there if they are simply learned and followed. One of them is logical data modeling.

Computer-based systems have become increasingly complex over the past decades, and that trend will continue. In the past, one of the project manager's responsibilities was to keep the *vision* of the overall system *in his/her mind,* thus ensuring that all the components of an application remained faithful to the purpose of the system. That is no longer possible given today's large and complex systems. The vision must reside elsewhere. The model has become the new *keeper of the vision.*

USING MODELS TO BUILD SYSTEMS

A *model* is an abstract representation of a subject that looks and/or behaves like all or part of the original. The model can be physical, such as a mockup of the Space Shuttle; graphical, such as a drawing or blueprint of a building; or conceptual, such as the mathematical formulas used for weather forecasting (Table 1.1).

Table 1.1 Types of Models

MODEL TYPE	CHARACTERISTICS
Physical	• An identical, smaller, or larger copy of an object. • Example: A full-size mockup of the cockpit of an airplane.
Graphical	• A diagram, drawing, or pictogram that is an abstract representation of a real, or potentially real, thing. • Example: A drawing or blueprint of a house.
Mathematical	• A conceptual construct using mathematics or a mathematical or formal language. • Example: A set of equations used for predicting weather patterns.

Modeling is the process of creating the abstract representation of a subject.

In today's computer-based world, the vision of an overall system is a series of models that represents the processes, data, and movement of information throughout an organization. These models are often graphical—residing on paper as text and diagrams or in machines.

Why Use Models?

Imagine you have a new job recording family histories for a local ancestry project. Your assignment is to interview a woman named Marie and record her family history. You sit down with

Marie and ask her questions about her family. Below are your notes.

> Marie was born in 1986. Her parents are Richard and Sofia. Her maternal grandparents were Robert and Julia, who were married in 1954. Robert died in 2010. They had two daughters, Sara (born in 1955) and Sofia (born in 1959). Sara married Frank and adopted a daughter Anna before divorcing in 1989. Marie's paternal grandparents were Francis and Angela, who married in 1951. Francis died in 2010. They had two children, Richard (born in 1959) and Laura (born in 1953). Laura gave birth to a daughter Rose in 2005 before she divorced in 2008 and died in 2020. Richard married Sofia in 1982. They had two children, Marie (born in 1986) and Andy (born in 1990). Julia died in 2012 and Frank in 1988.

Your job, as a family history interviewer, is similar to the job of a business or systems analyst interviewing users for a new account management system. Both family history interviewer and analyst sit down with the interviewee and listen to her, with an occasional probing or clarifying question thrown in, as they simultaneously try to take accurate notes. When the interview session is over, they go back to their desks and transcribe the chicken-scratch notes into a coherent and legible report, all the while documenting any errors, omissions, or questions. Then comes another trip to the interviewee to fix the errors, fill in the omissions, and answer the new questions. Then back to the office and the cycle repeats as many times as necessary until all the important information is documented or until the interviewee's patience runs out.

Lucky for you, just before trekking off to the interview, a colleague hands you a copy of *Genograms: Assessment and Intervention*,[2] which presents a simple system, using graphical symbols, to diagram a family history. For example, a square represents a male while a circle is used for a female. A horizontal line between two people indicates a relationship. A vertical line shows progeny. An X through the circle or square indicates that the person is dead.

Using these and a few more symbols, Marie's family genogram might look something like Figure 1.1.

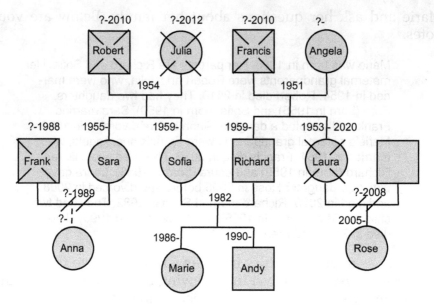

Figure 1.1 A Genogram

Reviewing Marie's genogram raises a few obvious questions:

Who did Laura marry?

When was Frank born?

When was Anna born?

Is Angela still alive?

…as well as a few not so obvious questions…

Did Laura really have a child at age 52?

…and a glaring error.

Frank could not have died a year before his divorce.

Using the genogram has a number of advantages. First, it can re-place note taking. You can start drawing the diagram as Marie talks. Second, the information is probably more accurate because diagramming is often faster than writing, allowing more time for listening to the interviewee, thus allowing you to immediately

4

catch and correct omissions, such as asking Marie about missing birthdates. Third, errors are more obvious and can often be found during the interview, such as Frank's post-mortem divorce. Fourth, you can show the diagram, even a rather crude hand-drawn one, to the interviewee during the interview for immediate feedback, reducing or eliminating follow-up interviews.

More generally, genograms are superior to handwritten notes for four important reasons. If properly executed, Genograms are:

- *Accurate.* They can increase the verity of information transferred from interviewee to interviewer.

- *Efficient.* They can reduce the time required to complete an effective interview.

- *Teachable.* Virtually anyone can learn how to create them with just a few hours of (self-) instruction.

- *Expandable.* Additional concepts are easily added, such as family member behavior (abusive, manipulative, estranged, etc.), health (heart disease, Alzheimer's, diabetes, etc.), and relationships (divorced, foster child, twins, etc.).

The lessons learned doing family histories should be obvious to anyone who must interview people to document any subject (family history, business process, or computer-based application). Models just make sense.

Traditional Roles of Models in Systems Development—Logical and Physical

Since at least the 1960s, if not before, systems developers recognized there was merit to understanding *what* the user wanted before delving into *how* to do it. Building a house starts with a blueprint and not with pouring concrete. Aircraft are designed on paper before any assembly work commences. One can imagine the pyramids on papyrus before the first stone was cut. Systems developers simply follow what has worked for so many other building projects for thousands of years. Today, this separation of work is called the *logical/physical distinction*. House plans, aircraft blueprints, and pyramid papyruses are abstract models of what will be physically constructed. Abstract representations are referred to as *logical models*.

Take the example of building a house. The start of the process is a picture of what the house should look like. This picture would show the location and general size of the bedrooms and kitchen and where the house sits on the land. The *logical design* of the house is the first phase of the building project.

The second project phase is the architect's plans. The picture created in logical design now becomes measurements showing electrical wiring, plumbing, and the coordinates of the structure. This is the *physical design* phase of the project.

The third phase is ordering the lumber, hiring the carpenters, laying the bricks, painting the walls, etc., the *construction* phase (Figure 1.2).

Figure 1.2 Development Cycle

These three phases—logical design, physical design, and construction—are the core of all building projects, be they houses, airplanes, or computer-based payroll systems.

In systems development, *logical design*[3] is concerned with conceptual constructs, while *physical design* is involved with introducing hardware, software, networks, and the like that work to accomplish what was defined in the logical design (Table 1.2). During *construction*, the phase that follows physical design, the computer code is written. In the broadest sense, logical design focuses on *what* is needed—the statement of the situation or the problem to be solved. Physical design is concerned with *how* logical design is accomplished. Construction makes the *how* a reality. Unfortunately, in spite to thousands of years of history, systems developers sometimes confuse the three.

Table 1.2 Logical Design,
Physical Design, and Construction Concerns

LOGICAL DESIGN	PHYSICAL DESIGN	CONSTRUCTION
• What does the end user need? • What do users want/expect?	• How will the system deliver the required services? • How should the hardware and software be configured?	• Building (coding) the actual application • Building (schema design) the actual database

A few developers have trouble separating design from construction, but the real problem is separating logical from physical design.

Logical design should be separated from physical design for three very important reasons. Logical design:

•   Deals with different subject matter—the *what*, not the *how*.

•   Is performed at a different time—the *what* must be understood before the *how* can be identified.

•   Requires different skills (interviewing, researching, analyzing) than those used in other phases.

Some people believe that although the distinction between the *what* and the *how* is relevant, that the division need not be taken too seriously. In other words, identifying both simultaneously is perfectly all right, and specifying database design options during logical data modeling is an acceptable practice. This perspective can lead to a serious problem because a major cause of poor design is the failure to completely understand *what* is desired—not *how* to implement it. Not convinced? Ask a few end users. Study after study has shown that a major user complaint about IT is that it does not listen to what users are saying.

Allowing logical designers to wander into physical solutions encourages them to shortcut the complete specification of the problem. When the problem is not completely understood, an acceptable and useful solution is doubtful.

The safest way to ensure that the physical design is complete and accurate is to guarantee that the problem, or the *what*, is completely and thoroughly understood. This message is reinforced throughout this book: *First, thoroughly and completely understand and document* what *is needed. Then, and only then, examine* how *to implement it.*

Traditional Roles of Models in Systems Development—Process and Data

In systems development, there are two main types of models: process models and data models.

Process Models

A *process model* is the representation of the processes, functions, and procedures in a user or systems environment.

Some process models focus on understanding *what* the user wants while others on *how* to deliver what is wanted. The *what* is represented by analysis or requirements techniques such as data-flow diagramming and use-case analysis.

Using these methods, techniques, and tools, developers build a *logical process model*—a logical picture of the organization's processes—consisting of the interactions among the objects in the organization and with the outside world (Figure 1.3a). Physical issues, such as hardware and software, are postponed until later. Once the developer understands and documents *what* the end user wants, then attention turns to *how* to deliver the desired system. Using techniques such as flow charts and state-transition diagrams during the *physical design* task, developers construct a *physical process model* (Figure 1.3b). Programmers can then use this model as a guide for coding the application in the construction phase (Figure 1.3c).

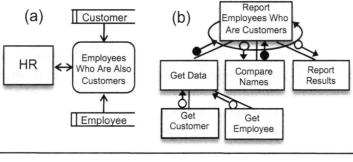

Figure 1.3 (a) Logical Process Model,
(b) Physical Process Model (c) Construction

Disciplined process analysis and process design techniques are excellent if the objectives are to understand the processes of an organization and to translate them into the directions that a programmer needs to write code. However, as good as these techniques are, they are incomplete. What is missing is the equally important emphasis on data.

Data Models

A *data model* is the representation of the definition, characterization, and relationships of data in a user or systems environment.

While process modeling documents the organization's processes, *data modeling* documents the organization's data. As with process modeling, *logical data modeling* documents *what* the user wants while *physical data modeling* documents *how* to deliver what the use wants.

As with process modeling, there a numerous data methods, techniques, and tools to accomplish data modeling. The *what* is documented using logical data modeling techniques, such as the Entity-Relationship Model[4] (Figure 1.4a). Physical data modeling shows *how* the data needs to be stored and accessed (Figure 1.4b). Database schema designers can then merge the physical models with the rules, characteristics, and limitations of a particular database management or file system to construct the actual database (Figure 1.4c).

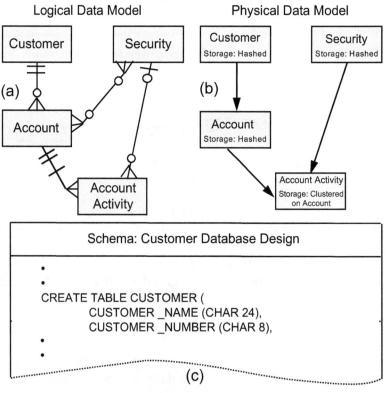

Figure 1.4 (a) Logical Data Model,
(b) Physical Data Model (c) Database Schema

Data models present a picture of an organization's data and the information the processes need to perform their function. Only when you have both—processes and data—is there a complete picture of the organization or the computer-based system.

Why Data Modeling Is Needed

Why is data modeling needed? The main reason is that systems developers are so bad at building files and databases. Perhaps that is an exaggeration, but it is true that developers look to techniques such as data modeling to enhance less-than-perfect application development skills.

In addition, although development organizations are under increasing pressure to integrate applications, attempts at integration using application code have proved to be slow, expensive, and overly complex. Because integration using data has been more successful, the need for and importance of data modeling has grown significantly. Data can be the glue that ties together otherwise disparate applications. However, with data integration comes the burden of not only understanding the data needed for just one application, but also knowing how the application's data fit into the larger organization.

Developers model data to ensure that they understand:

- *The user's perspective of data.* Data modeling, like process modeling, makes the distinction between the logical concept of *what* the user wants and the physical concept of *how* the system should provide it. In modeling the data, the developer uses a standard approach to capture facts about information and to verify and communicate those facts to the necessary parties.

- *The independence of data from their use.* By separating the data from processes, the basic definitions and characteristics of the data an organization needs are isolated from changes in processes, physical storage techniques, media, and access methods.

- *How data are used across applications.* Data modeling makes integration across applications easier by keeping track of data definitions, lifecycle information (who creates, updates, reads, and destroys data), and how and when data are used.

In fact, when properly applied, data modeling helps the developer:

- *Safeguard against duplication.* Data models help identify who uses the same data, when, and where. Applying this knowledge can ensure that the database does not mistakenly store the same information in multiple places.

- *Reduce inflexibility.* By separating the definition of the data from their use, data modeling reduces the chance that small changes to data or processes will cause large and expensive changes in applications and databases.

- *Eliminate inconsistency.* Even without duplicate data, inconsistencies can occur (e.g., updating a customer's payment history without also updating the customer's credit status). Data modeling permits the developer to modify one piece of data without fear of contradicting another.

The logical data model is a major source of information for physical database design. It provides the physical database designer with the information he or she needs to make the tradeoffs that are so important to an efficient physical database design. (Physical database design tradeoffs are discussed in Chapter 7.)

However, the logical data model also plays an important role after a project is complete. When properly maintained and kept up to date, the logical data model allows future changes to computer programs or data to be accurately and efficiently applied to the database. It also reduces or eliminates the need to recreate the logical data model every time an application is modified or a new one started.

Physical Database Design

Physical database design is concerned with constructing information platforms (databases or files). It does this using the logical data model, the logical process model, the physical data model, and the physical process model to create a database suitable for a specific systems environment (hardware, software, network). For example, a physical database designer might be charged with using the data and process models for a payroll system to generate the computer commands to create an Oracle payroll database.

The physical database designer is, therefore, a user of the models. The models become a communications tool that allows the designer to understand, in a standardized format, how end users see and use their data (Figure 1.5).

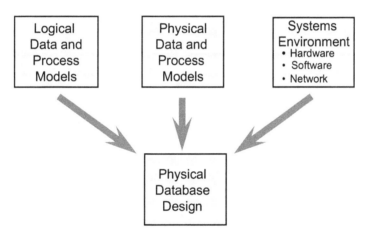

Figure 1.5 Physical Database Design

Physical database design and the associated application programs are the culmination of the entire modeling effort.

How Data Modeling Is Organized

In decades past, the term "data model" was used with modifiers such as hierarchical, network, inverted, relational, or object-oriented to describe the type or classification of a database management system. Such modifiers are rarely used today. For many developers, data model and logical data model are synonymous.

For purposes of this book, *data model* applies to both the logical and physical structure of data, and *data modeling* refers to the study of any state of data from its logical representation (such as with an Entity-Relationship diagram) through physical design (such as a data structure chart), to construction (a database schema).

Because data modeling can represent data anywhere on their journey from the very abstract to a field in a database, it can best be described as a continuum with the ethereal or abstract at one end of the scale and the very concrete at the other end (Figure 1.6). Any points in between are just that, points in between the start and end of a lifecycle.

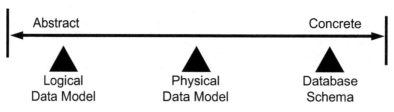

Figure 1.6 Data-Modeling Continuum

This is a somewhat more robust definition of data modeling than many people use. Analysts focus on the logical aspects of data and, therefore, see data modeling as only logical. Physical database designers have a view of data at the more physical end of the spectrum. However, data modeling is, in reality, much more inclusive than either of those two perspectives, which is one reason why data modeling language can seem confusing.

LOGICAL DESIGN PRINCIPLES

Any serious area of study or practice needs a clear vision and realistic goals incorporated into a set of principles that aid and guide practitioners to a successful conclusion. These guiding principles need to follow recognized axioms, and be complete, consistent with industry best practices, and provide a clear understanding of the subject.

Three overriding *Logical Design Principles* drive successful data modeling.

One: The Separation Principle—*Separate logical design from physical design.* A simple concept that states: understand *what* needs to be done before figuring out *how* to do it. It is the fundamental, disciplined, and near universal formula for all systems development.

Two: The Distinction Principle—*Distinguish logical data modeling from logical process modeling.* All data definitions, characteristics, and relationships need to be analyzed, designed, and documented in a manner that captures their relevant information. For logical data modeling, that means independent of any use.

Three: The Communication Principle—*Clearly deliver information requirements to both users and technical staff in a manner most useful to each.* Requirements must be clearly stated and understandable by all audiences, providing detail that illuminates.

Each is discussed in detail below.

The Separation Principle. *Separate logical design from physical design.*

This simple concept has been ignored, neglected, and corrupted by some of the best minds in the IT industry. The principle is: know *what* you need to do before you figure out *how* to do it. This principle is in response to the oldest and most severe criticism users have of IT—IT does not listen to what users want.

This oldest systems development principle, discovered long before the first commercial computer was invented, is also the most poorly communicated one.

Lack of understanding is the major complaint users have with systems developers—and the users are probably right. More important, projects that are not well grounded in what the user wants are suspect and likely to fail. Consultants have become rich replacing in-house developers who have not adequately, or to user satisfaction, understood *what* is wanted.

One of the major causes of poor understanding of requirements is the propensity of systems developers to jump into the physical design stage prematurely. Generally, this occurs for one of two reasons:

- Cutting corners owing to the false belief that the user requirements are already sufficiently understood so a detailed study is unnecessary.

- Impatience or pressure to move on to systems building.

Both of these reasons can limit or misdirect the options that the project can pursue.

Cutting Corners

Granted, some people just like to cut corners to make life easier. However, most analysts cut comers for the best of reasons, such as to avoid wasting time doing analysis that seems obvious or where the outcome is already determined.

Surprisingly, the amateurs or new systems developers are often the ones guilty of cutting corners. Take the example of commercial airline pilots. It is the seasoned captains who are the meticulous checklist followers, chiding newer pilots who attempt shortcuts. The same is true in systems development, it is the seasoned professionals who are more likely to *do it by the book* than their neophyte teammates.

Coming up with a Premature Solution

When investigating a problem, it is hard to put out of mind that flash of genius about how the database should be implemented. What should be done? Well, specifying a solution at this point is wrong because:

- Not all the data are in, so the complete picture might dictate a different solution from the one conceived when only part of the problem was uncovered.

- Others reviewing the model will not be able to understand why the solution solves the problem because the problem has not been completely stated.

This does not mean that analysts should purge their minds of solutions. Good ideas are hard enough to come by without throwing them away. When a clever idea surfaces, it should be written down and passed along to the physical designers at the right time, which, all now realize, is after logical design.

Systems Development Lifecycle

The traditional way of looking at the systems development lifecycle is linear. Development is a progression of logical design to physical design to construction (coding and testing to implementation)—a sequence of phases referred to as the waterfall approach (Figure 1.7a). Each phase stands alone and is completed before moving on to the next. Going back to a previous phase is an indication that the developers missed something and need to correct a mistake or oversight.

The do-logical-first tenet has been supplemented, if not replaced, with many newer systems development approaches. Iterative and incremental systems development techniques, such as rapid prototyping, agile development, low code, and DevOps, divide the system into a number of pieces, with each one going through a number of small cycles of analysis, design, and coding (Figure 1.7b). For example, imagine a user sitting down with a systems developer to create, "on the fly," application reports or input screens. The user indicates what is wanted, and the developer mocks up the screen. The cycle of the user recommending some feature, commenting on work completed, or pointing out errors, is repeated as many times as necessary until user and developer are satisfied with the result.

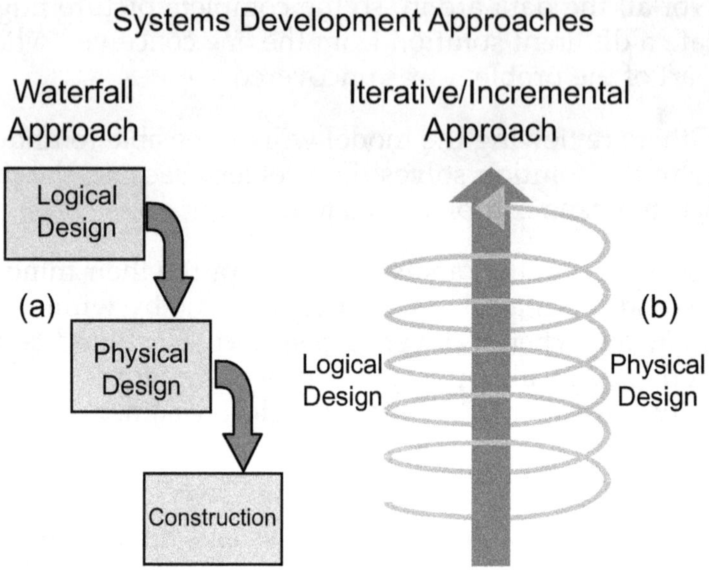

Systems Development Approaches

Waterfall
Approach

Iterative/Incremental
Approach

Logical
Design

(a)

(b)

Physical
Design

Logical
Design

Physical
Design

Construction

Figure 1.7 Systems Development Approaches
(a) Waterfall and (b) Iterative/Incremental

Some developers believe that iterative and incremental techniques replace analysis and design, but they are mistaken. Whether logical design is a single 6-month phase, as in the waterfall approach, or multiple 2-week iterations in agile development, or even 2-minute iterations in the screen development example, the principle is the same—understand *what* is wanted before specifying *how* to do it.

The Separation Principle: Real World Corollary

There is a corollary to the Separation Principle called the Real World Corollary.

Real World Corollary (a) A logical design is valid if, and only if, it reflects the real (user) world, and (b) A logical design is invalid if it contains non-real (user) world objects or concepts. Invalid objects and concepts include elements belonging in physical design or construction (such as keys, pointers, and disk drives).

This corollary reinforces the point that the purpose of logical design is to document the real world, which, in this context, is the user world.

Think of the Separation Principle as data modeling's *Prime Directive*—model the organization, not the technology.

The Distinction Principle. *Distinguish logical data modeling from logical process modeling.*

The *Distinction Principle* calls for the differentiation, not separation, of logical data modeling from logical process modeling. What's the difference?

Like it or not, the two tasks, data modeling and process modeling, are different. What the logical data modeler has to do to gather the information an organization needs or uses is different from what the logical process modeler needs to do. The need for different techniques, training, and skills means that the two tasks, regardless of who performs them, are always going to be seen as disjointed. It might not be ideal, but it is the reality of the situation.

Five characteristics distinguish logical data modeling from logical process modeling.

- *Processes are dynamic by nature, while data are typically static.* When users talk about their workplace, they usually focus on organizational processes. The picture they paint is one of movement and action, e.g., invoices arrive, orders are taken, and products are shipped to customers. Process modeling must record these movements, and the processes they describe generally have action-oriented names such as "Validate Customer Credit Status" or "Calculate Balance." By contrast, data are quite static. A customer name does not move or initiate some change or action.

- *Processes are more volatile than data.* The processes in an organization are more prone to change than data, and they typically change at a much faster rate. The way an organization processed orders last year is not necessarily the way they process them this year, and no one knows how they will be processed next year. Given this constant evolution of processes, process-modeling techniques must be able to accommodate frequent change. However, the data an organization uses, or, more accurately, the definition of the data an organization uses, changes far less frequently. Even when data do change, the change is more likely to affect only a few objects, not masses of objects, as often occurs with process changes. This difference caused one pundit to quip, "data ages like wine, processes age like fish." By separating the documentation of volatile processes from the more stable data, the changes in one area are less likely to affect the other area.

- *Physical database designers need different information than application programmers.* Process modeling does an admirable job of conveying to systems designers what the computer programs must do, such as information about the changes data must undergo to, for example, "suspend a customer." However, process models do a less effective job of conveying to physical database designers what the database must do. Physical database designers need information about the relationships between data objects (e.g., a customer can have multiple addresses) and how a change to one object might affect other objects (e.g., when a customer is deleted, the address of the customer must also be deleted).

- *Data require a data-oriented, not process-oriented, method of documentation.* Although process modeling effectively describes real-world processes, it does not do as well with real-world data. Process modeling techniques, such as data-flow diagrams and structure charts, do a good job expressing the richness of process dynamics. However, these techniques do not adequately describe the richness of the data. Data need a modeling approach that emphasizes their focus and characteristics (Table 1.3). Information specific to data items includes who creates it, what it looks like, how long it should exist, and how it changes over time.

Table 1.3 Process Versus Data Characteristics

PROCESSES	DATA
• Dynamic (involves movement) • They change frequently • Principal user is the programmer • Best documentation methods show algorithms, movement of data, and flow of control	• Static • The definition rarely changes • Principal user is the physical database designer • Best documentation methods show data definitions and data relationships

• *The skills and career choices of the analysts who perform process and data modeling are often different.* This is an unfortunate reason that data modeling is different from process modeling; but, because this book was written for the practitioner in the corporate trenches and not for the academic researcher, it is both real and unavoidable for at least the foreseeable future.

In most organizations, two different teams perform the two modeling tasks. A process team is trained in the techniques and tools of process modeling, and a separate data team is trained in data-related techniques and tools. Why? Go into any team room and ask the developers about their training. However you measure training, be it college courses, seminars, or just reading books, the amount of process expertise the average team member has been exposed to can be 10 times the amount of data expertise. Many individuals trained in process modeling are simply not comfortable doing data modeling. They don't understand it, don't see the need for it, or simply don't want to be part of it. Perhaps it is the result of the heavy focus on computer programming in college IT courses or a legacy from writing programs on their home computer in high school, but the majority of systems development professionals are process and not data focused.

Consequently, like it or not, if an IT shop wants to have an acceptable information platform supporting its applications, then it needs to have a team dedicated to data. Maybe someday this will change. It certainly is the objective of object technology enthusiasts. Nevertheless, for the time being, a substantial skill wall divides process and data.

However, the two teams do need to communicate and coordinate their efforts. The deliverables of each team, while they need to reflect the work of the other, also need to be independent of each other.

The Communication Principle. *Clearly deliver information requirements to both end users and technical staff in a manner most useful to each.*

Requirements must be clearly stated, understandable by all audiences, end-user oriented, and consist of detail that illuminates.

The major purpose of logical data modeling is to communicate the end-user view of the organization's data to those who will design the physical system. However, the communication principle is not only applicable to end users. Many people of differing backgrounds and skills need to understand the logical data model (Table 1.4).

Table 1.4 Groups Who Need to Understand the Data Model

GROUP	NEED TO
• End user • Systems analyst • Database administrator and physical database designers • Analysts working on other projects	• Affirm or correct the data represented on the logical data model. • Understand the data used in the logical process models. • Understand how the end user sees data so their needs can be accurately represented in the database design. • See how this project defines data so that interfaces can be developed and data shared across applications.

When developing the logical data model documents and diagrams, the goal is clarity. The intention is to communicate. When adding information to the data model, the modeler must ask, "Is this information adding to our understanding of the organization or subtracting from it?" This does not mean that the model should not be, or need not be, detailed, but rather that what is needed is detail that illuminates, not clouds.

CHAPTER NOTES

[1]Michael Bloch, Sven Blumberg, and Jürgen Laartz, "Delivering Large-Scale IT Projects on Time, on Budget, and on Value," *Digital McKinsey*, October 2012.
Also in *McKinsey on Finance*, 2013 volume 45, pp. 28-35.

[2]Monica McGoldrick, Randy Gerson, and Sueli Petry, *Genograms: Assessment and Intervention* (3rd Edition), W. W. Norton and Company, 2008.

[3]The word *logical* in IT means non-physical or abstract. A computer can have one or more physical disk drives that can be configured as any number of logical disk drives. A physical file can be part of a larger logical file or made up of multiple smaller logical files. Link editors convert a computer program's logical memory addresses to physical memory addresses. The same is true for workstations, databases, and a large number of other IT objects. In IT, *logical* is contrasted with *physical*; where *logical* represents the conceptual or abstract and *physical* represents real things such as CPUs, disk drives, and workstations.

[4]Peter Chen, "The Entity-Relationship Model-Toward a Unified View of Data," *ACM Transactions on Database Systems*, 1,1 (March 1976), pp. 9-36.

When developing the logical data model, documents, and diagrams, the goal is clarity. The intention is to communicate. When adding information to the data model, the modeler must ask: Is this information adding to our understanding of the organization or subtracting from it? This does not mean that the model should not be "detailed," but rather, that what is needed is detail that illuminates, not clouds.

CHAPTER NOTES

Richard Sharpe, Tom Johnston, and Birgen Hoertz. "Delivering Large-Scale IT Projects on Time, on Budget, and on Value." 2012.

[illegible entry] Company 2016.

[illegible entries]

[illegible]

Tom Johnston. "The Why" [Relationship Matters]: [Why] It Is Defined, Data" ACM Transactions on Database [Systems] 12 (1)(Mar): 9-36.

Chapter
2

Entities and Attributes

When we mean to build, we first survey the plot, then draw the model.
~ Shakespeare

A noble, logical diagram once recorded will never die.
~ Daniel H. Burnham (architect)

Logical data modeling depicts, organizes, and catalogs the data objects an organization uses in its every day work. *Entities* and *attributes* are the two most fundamental *data objects*.

- *Entities* are persons, places, or things about which an organization wants to save information. Employees, States, Orders, and Time Sheets are examples of entities.

- *Attributes* are the properties of entities. Attribute examples include COLOR, NAME, EMPLOYMENT DATE, and SOCIAL SECURITY NUMBER.

The following sections deal with each object in detail.

ENTITIES

Entities are the basic standalone information components of an organization. They are the things that immediately come to mind when thinking about a topic. If the subject is schools, then it is teachers, students, classes, buildings, and classrooms. If the subject is retail stores, then the focus is customers, products, warehouses, and displays.

Entity Names and Definitions

It is important to distinguish one entity from another. The way to do this is to ensure that each entity has a unique name. Data modeling requires the strictest definition of unique. No two entities can have the same name. If a company makes a distinction between employees and former employees, requiring two distinct entities, then those two entities need two different names, such as Current Employee and Former Employee.

As a convention, entity names have initial capital letters, can be as long as necessary, and can include multiple words, spaces, and special characters. If the entity name includes multiple words, then each word should start with a capital letter. For example, Customer might be a fine entity name for one organization while another might have two entities, Current Customer and Prospective Customer. Some authors recommend singular names for entities, although plural names are certainly acceptable, and suggested if they add clarity (Remember the Third Logical Design Principle: Communication.) For example, a school logical data model might include the singular case entities Teacher and Classroom, but the plural Students.

The *as long as necessary, multiple words, spaces allowed,* and *singular or plural* naming guidelines allow the modeler to avoid awkward and uncommunicative constructs such as trans_cust for Transient Customer or q_p-t_fin_proj for Quarterly Pre-Tax Financial Projections (that Third Logical Design Principle: Communication again).

There should be a robust, unique, and useful definition for each entity. For example, a business might define the entity Customer as follows:

> A Customer is an individual or organization that currently pur-
> chases, or has purchased within the last 10 years, goods or ser-
> vices.

A newspaper might see its customers as two separate entities, Transient Customers and Display Customers defined as follows.

> A Transient Customer is an individual or organization that places
> a single transaction ad in the paper, such as a classified ad sell-
> ing a car. Each ad generates an associated bill. The Account as-
> sociated with the ad is closed and deleted 60 days after the
> payment is received.

> A Display Customer is an organization that places multiple ads in
> the paper, is billed monthly, and may qualify for volume dis-
> counts. The Account associated with the ad remains open even
> after payment.

It is important to save the information about the entity in a safe place where it can be used and shared by all members of the organization. A *data dictionary* is a repository of detailed documentation and other useful information about logical and physical data objects. It is an integral part of data modeling. The dictionary can be as simple as a loose-leaf binder or as sophisticated as an automated library system. All entity documentation should be saved in a data dictionary.

This is an important point. A data model consists of two components: (1) a diagram graphically depicting the model and (2) a dictionary containing textual information about all data objects, whether represented on the diagram or not. Too many systems developers only think of the diagram when discussing the data model—a costly mistake.

Type/Occurrence Distinction

Before pressing on, the reader should understand the distinction between an entity *type* and an entity *occurrence* or *instance*. (*Occurrence* and *instance* are used interchangeably.) An *entity type* represents the class of objects that share a distinguishing factor. An *en-*

tity occurrence is a single case or example of a type. For example, Detective is an entity type, while "Sherlock Holmes," "Hercule Poirot," and "Ellery Queen" are instances of that entity type. Similarly, "1234," 5678," and "9012" can be instances of the entity type Invoice.

If this argument sounds familiar, it might be because you encountered it in a college philosophy class. Philosophers have what they call the *type-token distinction* where Man can represent the *set* or *type* of all men (and women—those ancient philosophers were rather chauvinistic devils), while Socrates represents a single *token* or *occurrence* of that set.

Entity instances are usually placed in double quotes. "Socrates" is an entity instance or occurrence of the entity type Greek Philosophers. In practice, the double quotes can be omitted if there is no risk of the reader confusing the type and the instance.

> The Type/Occurrence Distinction in data processing was not introduced with entities and attributes. It has existed for years in file and database design, where a file consists of a *record type* containing multiple *record occurrences*.

An entity occurrence or instance should always be identified as an occurrence or instance; however, the same is not always true for entity types. Some modelers abbreviate entity type to the simple word, entity. If no mention is made regarding whether the entity is a type or occurrence, it is usually assumed that it is a type. However, be careful. While this is a good rule of thumb, it cannot always be counted on. Data modelers often come across cases where the referent is an entity occurrence without the use of the word occurrence or instance. The second best differentiator of type and occurrence is context. The best differentiator is using initial caps for the type and double quotes for the instance.

Diagramming Entities

The graphical representation of an entity is a rectangular box (Figure 2.1).

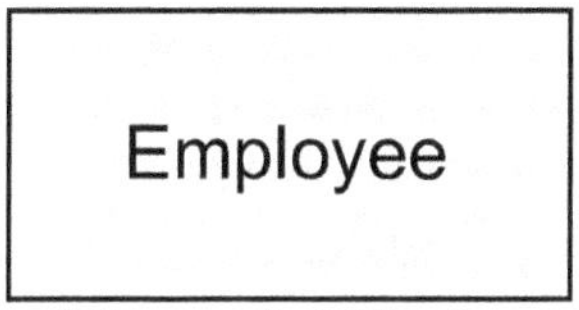

Figure 2.1 Entity

The entity name is placed in the rectangle.

ATTRIBUTES

Attributes are the properties of entities. For example, the entity Employee can have various properties such as employee name, data of birth, start date, department, pay grade, etc. The entity Car might have the attributes manufacturer, model, color, and manufacturing date. An easy way to tell attributes from entities is that attributes cannot stand alone—birth date and color are the properties of something and would not normally exist on their own.

Attributes are the most common data objects and certainly the ones most people think about when discussing data. They are also the oldest data objects, having a history before entities or files. Not surprisingly, their characteristics are the most robust of all the data objects.

To fully understand attributes the modeler must be familiar with the concepts *attribute name and definition, attribute type/occurrence, attribute value, attribute source, attribute complexity,* and *attribute valuation.*

Attribute Names and Definitions

As with entities, attributes need unique names and definitions.

As a convention, attribute names are in all capitals and can be as long as necessary, such as COLOR and LOCATION. The name can include multiple words and spaces as in DATE OF BIRTH and COUNTRY OF ORIGIN, as well as special characters. Although most names are singular, plural names are acceptable if they add clarity.

Type/Occurrence Distinction

As with entities, we can speak of *attribute types* and *attribute occurrences*. An attribute type is the set of all objects that are a single property of an entity. An attribute occurrence is a single case of an attribute type. For example, if the color of a car is blue, then car is the *entity*, color is the *property* of that entity, and blue is an *instance* of that attribute. An attribute *instance* or *occurrence* is given a special name and is called an *attribute value*.

An *attribute value* is a characteristic or fact about an entity occurrence. The fact might be that the entity's COLOR is "blue," or that the AUTHOR NAME is "Thomas Rowley." Attribute values are displayed in double quotes. They form the core of information management and represent the most tangible and least abstract aspects of all data processing.

If the word attribute is used without reference to it being a type or a value, then type is assumed. One hard and fast rule is to place attribute types in all caps. Without the use of all upper case letters, it is too easy to confuse an entity with an attribute.

WARNING! If you run across an old programmer—or if you are an old programmer—you might think that an attribute name needs to be unique only within an entity. In other words, two attributes can have the same name as long as they are not in the same entity. This is not true in data modeling. Every attribute needs a unique name.

An attribute should exist as a property of one and only one entity. Duplicate attributes are not allowed. This requirement can put pressure on the modeler to come up with unique attribute names. Some attributes are more problematic than others. The attribute name for an employee number is relatively easy to name (EMPLOYEE NUMBER), but some logical data models can have more than a dozen attributes referring to a date or a status code. The modeler must come up with a unique name for each one. The attribute name should reflect a legitimate, standalone data object and the name should not reference any entity or relationship. For example, EMPLOYEE NAME is an appropriate attribute name, while Employee.NAME (a concatenation of the entity Employee and the attribute NAME) is not.

For the most part, attribute definitions tend to be thin soup—there is usually not much there. How would you define COLOR? In most cases, it is rather straightforward—color is color. In some cases, however, it might be more complex. For example, the definition of COLOR might state that only natural colors are allowed or only those on a particular design palette. This descriptive information is placed in the data dictionary.

Although the actual attribute definition might be a bit short, attributes do tend to have considerable additional definitional baggage, as you will see below.

Domains

A *domain* is the set of possible attribute values that an attribute can have. Examples of domains include dates, text, integers between 200 and 399, real numbers with two decimal places, and state abbreviations (FL, NJ). However, while "July 11, 2021" is an acceptable value for EMPLOYMENT DATE, "fried toad" is not.

Domains are important because they not only identify the acceptable values of an attribute, but also how to use the attribute. For example, the following statement…

> MEDICAL COVERAGE = "YES" if CLAIM DATE is greater than or equal to EMPLOYMENT DATE and less than or equal to TERMINATION DATE

…only makes sense if the values for…

- CLAIM DATE
- EMPLOYMENT DATE
- TERMINATION DATE

…all share the same domain. If…

- CLAIM DATE = "May 5, 2020"
- EMPLOYMENT DATE = "July 11, 2019"
- TERMINATION DATE = "123 South Main Street"

…the results will be, as they say, unpredictable.

Domains can be very specific or quite generic. Generic domains, such as integer, text, or the ever popular alphanumeric (which excludes little), are the easiest to work with but also the least meaningful. Domains such as *Dates between 1/1/2010 and 12/31/2050* or *Official Postal Codes* are more useful.

Domains can be nested, that is, the scope of one domain can incorporate another. The domain *Dates between 1/1/2001 and 12/31/2025* is incorporated in the domain *Dates*, which is incorporated in the domain *Integers*, and so on.

For purposes of clarity, one can speak of three types of domains:

- A *data type* is a programming language term that identifies broad domain categories, such as Integers, Real Numbers, Text, and U.S. Dollars.

- *Ranges*, such as Dates Between 1/1/2010 and 12/31/2050, Nonnegative Values Between 0 and 4.0, and Last Names Beginning A To J, indicate that values between two end points are acceptable.

- *Acceptable values* list the only values an attribute can have. Postal Codes, State Names, and Presidents Of The United States would be examples of lists of acceptable values. The only acceptable values for a retail store CUSTOMER STATUS attribute might be "Active" and "Inactive."

In effect, a domain can be considered a hierarchy with the data type at the highest level and acceptable values at the lowest.

Each domain should have a unique name to distinguish it from other domains. As a convention, domain names use initial capital letters, can be as long as necessary, and can include multiple words, spaces, and special characters.

Attribute Source

It is important to know how an attribute relates to the organization. Attributes can contain information fundamental to the business, or they can be the result of some calculation carried about by the business, or they can be used to identify other information.

Attribute Source: Primitive and Derived

Attributes can be either *primitive* or *derived*.

A *primitive attribute* is one that expresses an *atomic* or nondecomposable fact (value) about the entity, as in the COLOR is "blue."

A *derived attribute* is calculated from one or more primitive attributes (atomic facts), or other derived attributes, by the application of an algorithm. For example, in the accounts receivable data shown in Table 2.1, INVOICE AMOUNT is derived, because it can be calculated by adding up the ITEM AMOUNT values.

Table 2.1 Derived Data
INVOICE

INVOICE NUMBER	INVOICE DATE	INVOICE AMOUNT
12345	11/23/2022	$150.79
45677	11/24/2022	$263.87
34632	11/24/2022	$146.58
34673	11/25/2022	$342.56

LINE ITEM

INVOICE NUMBER	PRODUCT	QUANTITY	ITEM AMOUNT
12345	W235	1	$12.34
12345	Q2342	1	$23.32
12345	WW3434	1	$74.13
12345	P343	1	$41.00
34632	Q2342	2	$46.63
34632	AE456	1	$99.95
•	•	•	•
•	•	•	•

Primitive attribute information is placed in the data dictionary, and the attribute is assigned to an entity on the E-R diagram. Derived data are placed in the data dictionary but should not be assigned to an entity or placed on the E-R diagram. This is because a derived data item needs an algorithm to define its value, and thus is closer to a process than it is to a data object. (Remember the Second Logical Design Principle, Distinction.) As such, process-modeling techniques are better able to define and describe this attribute. (This topic will be discussed in greater detail in Chapter 8.)

Attribute Source: Descriptor and Identifier

Attributes are either *descriptors* or *identifiers*.

Descriptors specify a characteristic of an entity instance. They are the standard, garden variety attributes, e.g., COLOR = "blue."

Identifiers are attributes that uniquely determine an entity instance, e.g., EMPLOYEE NUMBER = "090-7894."

Many entities will have at least one attribute that is an identifier, some more than one, while many others will not have any identifiers at all. For example, the Employee entity could have these attributes: EMPLOYEE NUMBER, EMPLOYEE NAME, and EMPLOYEE SALARY. EMPLOYEE NAME and EMPLOYEE SALARY are descriptor attributes because salary is probably never unique and name cannot be counted on to be unique. EMPLOYEE NUMBER should be unique and should be designated as an identifier.

WARNING! Some data modelers, in their desire to support the work of the physical database designers, take it upon themselves to jumpstart the process by assigning each entity an identifier. This is a mistake and violates the First Logical Design Principle: Separation—the Prime Directive. It is important that the modeler model what is in the organization and not what the modeler thinks should be there. Leave physical design to the physical designers.

Attribute Source: Compound or Concatenated Identifiers

An identifier need not be confined to a single attribute. It can also be a group of attributes called a *compound identifier*, also called a *concatenated identifier*. The attributes ACCOUNT NUMBER and DATE may both be required to identify an interest payment to a bank account. Leaving one of these attributes out would make the identifier non-unique. If there is a chance that two interest payments could be posted to the same account on the same day, then another attribute, such as TIME, would have to be added to the compound identifier. However, including multiple unique identifiers in the compound identifier, e.g., including both a SOCIAL SECURITY NUMBER and EMPLOYEE NUMBER, is not necessary or recommended. If both are individually unique, then each is an identifier in its own right.

Be wary of identifiers consisting of long strings of attributes. In most every case, this is an attempt to create a natural (business) identifier where none exists.

Remember, this is not physical design. If an identifier exists in the organization (whether a single or compound identifier), document it. However, if an identifier is not part of the organization, then there should not be one in the logical data model. The job of the data modeler is to document fact not fiction.

Attribute Complexity

Attributes can be as simple as COLOR = "red" or considerably more complex. It is important for the modeler to identify both.

Attribute Complexity: Simple

A *Simple Attribute,* also called an *atomic attribute,* does not contain any other attributes. It is the *basic* or *fundamental* attribute that is the vast majority of the data in any data model.

Attribute Complexity: Group

A *Group Attribute* contains a fixed number of other attributes. For example, the attribute EMPLOYEE NAME could represent the group of attributes, LAST NAME, FIRST NAME, and MIDDLE INITIAL.

EMPLOYEE ADDRESS might contain the attributes, EMPLOYEE STREET NUMBER, EMPLOYEE STREET NAME, EMPLOYEE

CITY, EMPLOYEE STATE/PROVINCE, EMPLOYEE POSTAL CODE, and EMPLOYEE COUNTRY.

Groups are important for two reasons: (1) they are often a central or fundamental part of the organization, and/or (2) they are how people in the organization speak. Normal professional discourse involves talk about employee addresses or names and not last name, first name, and middle initial.

Common modeler mistakes include modeling only the group attribute or the individual attributes making up the group. Both need to be modeled. For example, in the example above it is important to model both the group attribute EMPLOYEE ADDRESS and the individual attributes that make up the group (EMPLOYEE STREET NUMBER, EMPLOYEE STREET NAME, etc.)

POTENTIAL TERMINOLOGY TRAP

Group attributes appear under different names in other books and tools. A modeler might find them called group data items, aggregate groups, compound attributes, aggregates, and, unfortunately, groups.

One further point. In 99 percent of the cases, the group attribute will consist of simple attributes. In 1 percent of the cases, the group attribute is made up of other group attributes.

Attribute Valuation

So far, attributes have been considered the bearer of a simple value. However, this is not always the case.

Attribute Valuation: Single-Valued Attributes

The vast majority of attributes that the data modeler will encounter contain a single value such as "blue," "27," or "poached cantaloupe." Such an attribute is called a *single-valued attribute*.

Attribute Valuation: Multivalued Attributes

Multivalued attributes are attributes with more than one value. As an example, take the Employee entity and its attribute EMPLOYEE DEGREES. Smith might have only one degree, a "BS," while Jones has three degrees, "BS," "MA," and "PhD." In like manner, the attribute COLOR for the Car entity might have the value "gray" for a staid 21st-century car or the palette-busting "blue," "green," and "brown" for a 1950s car.

WARNING! Some modelers try to cheat the user by representing multivalued attributes as distinct attribute types. Attribute names such as COLOR1, COLOR2, COLOR3, etc. are dead giveaways that some modeling chicanery is afoot. This might be done because the data modeler assumes that the database management system that will house the data does not support multivalued attributes. Nice sentiment but misplaced. This is logical data modeling not physical database design. Remember, model the organization, not the technology.

WARNING! (1) Do not confuse attribute value with attribute valuation. An attribute value is an instance of an attribute type while attribute valuation tells you if the attribute is single or multiple valued. They are two very different things. (2) Multivalued attributes can have various other names in other books and magazines, such as repeating group and, unfortunately, the single word *group*.

Attribute Complexity and Valuation

Some modelers struggle to distinguish group attributes from multivalued attributes either because of their similarity or because some authors call both *groups*. Here is a simple rule of thumb. A *group attribute* contains a fixed number of attributes of various domains, while a *multivalued attribute* contains a variable number of values, but of the same domain (Table 2.2).

Table 2.2 Attribute Complexity and Valuation

VALUATION / COMPLEXITY	SINGLE-VALUED	MULTIVALUED
SIMPLE	COLOR = "blue"	EMPLOYEE DEGREES = "BS," "MS," PhD"
GROUP	DATE consists of MONTH, DAY, YEAR	EXAM DATES = "1/15/2021," "5/15/2021," "8/15/2021

Making data modeling even more interesting, group attributes and multivalued attributes can be nested, e.g., a group attribute could have multiple values. For example, the group attribute EDUCATION could contain the attributes, UNDER GRADUATE and GRADUATE, with the latter containing the multivalued attribute DEGREES EARNED.

Diagramming Attributes

Attributes are diagrammed in many different ways or not diagrammed at all. Some modelers place attributes in the entity box, while others use ovals to hold attribute names (Figure 2.2).

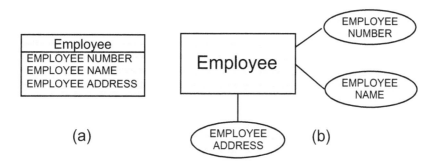

Figure 2.2 Diagramming Attributes:
(a) In the Entity Box, (b) In Ovals.

However, most modelers do not place attributes on the E-R diagram at all. The issue is space. Diagramming attributes only makes sense for simple models, for example those presented in textbooks or on classroom whiteboards, which have perhaps a dozen attributes in total. In the real world, E-R diagrams can quickly start to look like a Tokyo subway map as attributes are piled onto the page. A more practical approach is to keep attributes off the E-R diagram and in the data dictionary, the repository of documentation about the data model.

Chapter
3

Relationships

The relationship between the data is more important than the data.
~ James Burke

Assumptions are the termites of relationships.
~ Henry Winkler

Entities rarely, if ever, exist alone. In almost every case, an entity is related to, or associated with, one or more other entities. The entity School is usually associated with other entities such as Students, Teachers, Classroom, Course Name, etc. The entity Employee might be associated with the entities Department and Office Location. A *relationship* is a natural or end-user connection or association between entities. They are the glue that bonds entities together. Relationships are the third data object, along with entities and attributes, in a logical data model.

While entities very rarely exist without relationships, relationships cannot exist without being associated with at least one entity. Take the entities Customer and Car. Customers *buy* Cars so Buys is the relationship linking Customer and Car. Students *attend* School so Attends is the relationship between the entities Student and School. Buys and Attends never exist without being associated with some entity.

As with entities and attributes, there are *relationship types* and *relationship occurrences* or *instances*. Also, as with entities and attributes, if the relationship is not identified as an instance or occurrence, the modeler can assume it is a relationship type, but just to be careful, examine the context in which it is used.

Relationships are bidirectional, so if Customers do, in fact, Buy Cars then it is equally true that Cars Are Bought By Customers. Buys and Are Bought By are two separate labels for the same relationship.

Most important, a relationship describes an end-user association, not some technical one. Do not confuse the logical data modeling *relationship* with some physical database linkage. Remember: model the organization, not the technology.

Relationship Names and Definitions

Each relationship needs a unique name to distinguish it from all other relationships as well as other data modeling objects. As a convention, relationship names use initial capital letters, can be as long as necessary, and can include multiple words, spaces, and special characters. Relationship names are formally displayed in single quotes, although the quotes are not needed if the meaning is clear.

While modelers do a good job coming up with unique entity and attribute names, that is often not the case with relationships. There are far fewer unique relationship name candidates to choose from than with entities or attributes. For example, the model that includes 'Customers Buy Cars,' might also include 'Dealers Buy Parts.' Some modelers resolve the uniqueness problem by appending the entity names to the relationship name in the data dictionary, as in *Buy (Between Customer and Cars)* and *Buy (Between Dealer and Parts)*.

A phrase in the *entity-relationship-entity* construct, such as 'Customers Buy Cars' or 'Students Attend School,' is called an *entity-relationship pair*, which is a fashionable mechanism for representing many relationships. As a convention, entity-relationship pairs have initial capital letters and are set off in single quotes as in, 'Customers Buy Cars' or in 'Cars Are Bought By Customers.'

However, the quotes can be excluded if there is no chance of the reader mistaking the data modeler's intentions.

Diagramming Relationships

There are two options for representing a relationship on the E-R diagram: the line and the line with a diamond. The simplest way to represent a relationship is with a line (Figure 3.1a). Proper procedure is to place the relationship name on the line (Figure 3.1b). In some cases, to avoid confusion, it is recommended to label the relationship in both directions (Figure 3.1c). However, for various reasons, including time, space, and laziness, labeling in both directions is often not done. One good reason for not doing so is that it is often simply not needed if the meaning of the relationship is easily understood.

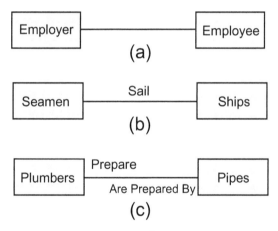

Figure 3.1 Relationship Conventions

A more traditional way to represent a relationship, and the one introduced by Peter Chen, the creator of the Entity-Relationship Model, is with a diamond bisecting a line. The name of the relationship is placed inside the diamond shape (Figure 3.2).

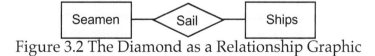

Figure 3.2 The Diamond as a Relationship Graphic

If you are using a data modeling software tool, you will find that some tools use the line, others the diamond, while still other tools allow the modeler to choose which to use. Either approach, using a line or diamond, is equally acceptable.

A special note. This book intentionally shifts back and forth between various diagramming conventions, thus forcing the reader to deal with different diagrammatic symbols. Hopefully, the exercise is worth the inconvenience. An ideal approach, but one beyond the control of this book, is a single standard set of diagrammatic conventions. Alas, the ideal is, at best, years away. For the time being, serious modelers must learn to recognize a number of different graphical conventions.

The distinction between a relationship name and relationship label is a subtle one. A relationship name identifies a single relationship between two or more entities, such as the relationship Bake in Bostonians Bake Beans. A relationship label is what is written on the E-R diagram.

With some diagramming tools, a single label is sufficient. (Figure 3.3a) Others require a label in each direction (Figure 3.3b). Both labeling techniques represent a single relationship.

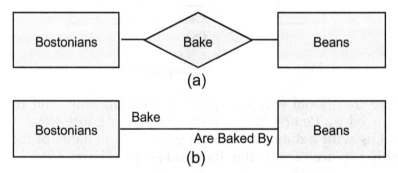

Figure 3.3 (a) A Single Relationship Label
(b) Labeling the Single Relationship in Both Directions.

By now, it is probably obvious that the simple entity-relationship pair, Customers Buy Products, is rather arbitrary and could just as easily be written Products Are Bought by Customers (Figure 3.4).

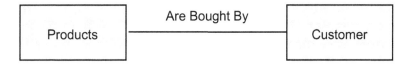

Figure 3.4 Labeling in Only One Direction

In practice, relationships are most commonly written in the active voice, Customers Buy Products, rather than in the passive voice, Products Are Bought by Customers. Readers tend to prefer the active voice, and, in most cases, the active voice involves fewer words, freeing up valuable diagram real estate.

Relationship Characteristics

Relationships have two characteristics that transform them from the most bland and lifeless of the three data objects, into the most rich and dynamic. These characteristics are *membership class* and *degree.*

Membership Class (Connectivity Characteristics)

Membership class describes how many occurrences of one entity type can relate to another entity type. The distinction between type and occurrence is important for understanding the membership class concepts of *cardinality* and *modality.*

To say that entity A is related to entity B is useful, but we want to know more. For example, it would be good to know how many A's are related to how many B's. Take the entity-relationship pair, Teachers Teach Students. It would be good to know how many students the teacher teaches. If every teacher teaches exactly 25 students, then that is useful—but it is also rare in information management. While everyone understands that a teacher teaches multiple students, the exact number is usually unknown and almost certainly unpredictable. When talking about the entity types Teachers and Students, the best we can say is that teachers teach *many* students.

If the exact number of A's related to B's is known, then that information needs to be documented in the data dictionary; however, in the vast majority of cases, the best we can say is that an occurrence of A is related to *zero, one,* or *many* occurrences of B. Zero, one, and many are the subject of membership class.

Membership Class: Cardinality

Cardinality is the specification of the maximum number of occurrences of one entity type that can be related to the one or more occurrences of another entity type.

Cardinality is expressed as simply *one* or *many.* For example, a husband can have only *one* wife (at least here in New Jersey), while a parent can have *many* children. In like manner, an Invoice can be related to *many* Line Items, but a Line Item can be related to only *one* Invoice. Taking into consideration all combinations of *one* and *many,* two entities can be related as:

- One-to-one (1:1)—An occurrence of entity A can, as a maximum, relate to one and only one occurrence of entity B, and an occurrence of B can relate, as a maximum, to only one occurrence of A. For example, a husband can have only one wife, and a wife only one husband.

- One-to-many (1:N)—One occurrence of entity A can relate, as a maximum, to many occurrences of entity B, but an occurrence of B can relate, as a maximum, to only one occurrence of A. For example, a mother can have many children, but a child can have only one mother.

- Many-to-many (M:N)—An occurrence of entity A can relate, as a maximum, to many occurrences of B, while an occurrence of B can relate, as a maximum, to many occurrences of A. For example, an uncle can have many nephews, while a nephew can have many uncles.

The cardinality represents the maximum number of occurrences, not the minimum. An uncle could legitimately be related to only one instance of a nephew or even none.

The most popular way to diagrammatically represent cardinality is to use the *bar* to express *one* and the *trident* (also called a *crow's foot*, *chicken foot*, or *fork*) to express *many* (Figure 3.5).

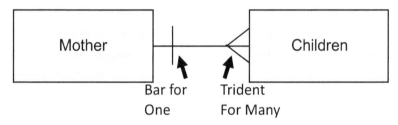

Figure 3.5 Cardinality

While the trident is currently the most popular graphic to represent a cardinality of many, it is not the only convention in use.

What this book calls the trident was first introduced by Gordon Evert in 1976 as an "inverted arrow."[1] In subsequent years, Evert revised the name to "fork," which is a good name but not widely accepted. Because the intent of this book is to use common terminology, it will focus on the term trident, but the developer should recognize that there are multiple names for the graphic, including crow's foot, chicken foot, and fork.

Chen represents cardinality by using a *1*, *N*, or *M* on the relationship line (standing for *one*, *many*, and *many*) (Figure 3.6).

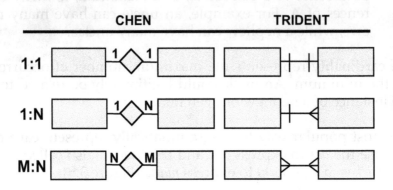

Figure 3.6 Diagramming Conventions

Most tools use the trident to show a cardinality of many, while some give the user a choice of symbols, including a dazzling array of circles, dots, horseshoes, and whatnot. All use either a bar or the character 1 to represent one.

It is acceptable to mix and match symbols, for example, a relationship depicted by a diamond and its cardinality represented by a trident or a relationship represented by a line with 1, N, or M for cardinality. However, simplicity and clarity would dictate minimizing the number of different symbols used on the E-R diagram.

Membership Class: Modality

The *modality* of a relationship indicates whether or not an entity occurrence *must* participate in a relationship. If an occurrence of entity A *must* relate to at least one entity occurrence B, then the modality is *mandatory*—there are no cases where an occurrence of A is not related to an occurrence of B. If an occurrence of entity A can relate to zero occurrences of entity B, then the modality is *optional*—an occurrence of A can but does not have to relate to an occurrence of B.

While *cardinality* indicates the maximum number of entity occurrences that *can* participate in a relationship (one or many), *modality* (also called *participation* or *optionality*) indicates the minimum number of occurrences (zero or one).

Take the example of Invoice and Line Item entities. An Invoice occurrence can relate to many Line Items, but a Line Item can relate to only one Invoice. This tells us the cardinality. However, is it possible to have a Line Item occurrence not related to an Invoice occurrence? The answer, of course, is "No." For a Line Item to exist, it must be linked to an Invoice. Therefore, the relationship is *mandatory* for the Line Item entity.

The same is true in the other direction. It makes no sense to have an Invoice without a Line Item. An Invoice must be related to at least one Line Item, so the relationship is *mandatory* in both directions (Figure 3.7).

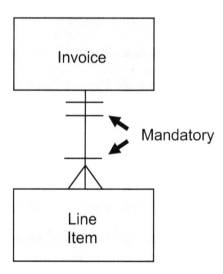

Figure 3.7 Mandatory Relationships

However, in the entity-relationship pair Gardeners Plant Trees, it is possible for a Gardener to have never planted a Tree just as it is possible for a Tree not to have been Planted by a Gardener. The relationship Plant is optional in both directions.

A *bar* represents a modality of *mandatory* (one) and a *circle* a modality of optional (zero). The boxes in Figure 3.8 indicate where the cardinality and modality symbols are located on the relationship line.

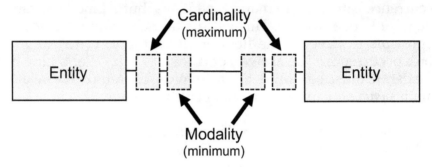

Figure 3.8 Cardinality/Modality

Look at the Artists Paint Pictures entity-relationship pair in Figure 3.9. Because it is not possible to have a picture without an artist, the relationship Pictures Are Painted by Artists is mandatory. However, it is possible to have Artists who are not related to any Pictures (just go to a Greenwich Village singles bar some Saturday night); therefore, in the other direction, the relationship is optional. Perhaps a better example is a sculptor who is an artist but his or her work is not a picture. When dealing with the modality of a relationship, modelers usually refer to the one end of a one-to-many relationship first. This relationship, then, is *mandatory-optional*.

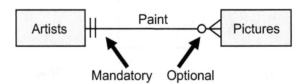

Figure 3.9 Mandatory-Optional Relationship
Using Trident Notation

Figure 3.10 shows the same entity-relationship-pair using Chen notation. Once again, the cardinality symbol (1, N, or M) is placed closest to the entity, while the modality symbol (0, 1) is placed inside the cardinality symbol.

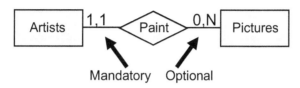

Figure 3.10 Mandatory-Optional Relationship
Using Chen Notation

By now some bright modelers might have noticed that the bar specifying a cardinality of one can usually be inferred, i.e., because a cardinality of zero is not possible (Figure 3.11a), and therefore, the bar is redundant (Figure 3.11b).

Figure 3.11 Cardinality (a) Cannot Be Zero
(b) Redundant Cardinality Bar

This is true, but the cardinality bar does serve a purpose. Because modelers do not always know the cardinality of a relationship, they must have a way to distinguish not knowing from knowing (Figure 3.12). In Figure 3.12b one knows that A and B are related one-to-one; in Figure 3.12a one simply does not know, or has not chosen to show, the cardinality.

Figure 3.12 Distinguishing (a) *Not Knowing*
From (b) a Cardinality of *One*

The relationship Banks Finance Cars is optional-optional because there are banks that do not finance cars, and there are cars that are not financed (Figure 3.13).

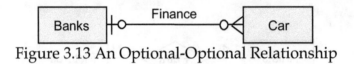

Figure 3.13 An Optional-Optional Relationship

A note on terminology: some data modelers use the term *optionality* instead of *modality*. This is an awkward and unfortunate use of the term because the optionality of a relationship could be either optional or mandatory. While an *optional optionality* appears redundant, it is not as bad as the seeming contradiction of a *mandatory optionality*.

Modality is a term taken from modal logic, where it is used to distinguish necessary statements (whose truth is necessary or mandatory) from contingent statements (whose truth is conditional or dependent on external conditions). Modality is, in fact, a more accurate, meaningful, and less confusing term than optionality, and the one used in this book.

Degree

Degree is the number of entity types participating in a relationship. The most common degree is *binary*, or relationships associated with just two entities. In Customers Buy Cars, Buy is in a binary relationship with entities Customers and Cars. The entity-relationship pair is an example of a binary relationship (Figure 3.14).

Figure 3.14 Binary Relationship

However, a relationship can also relate to more than two entities. Take the case of 'Customers Buy Cars from Dealers' (Figure 3.15). Here the relationship Buy links together three entities: Customers, Cars, and Dealers. A relationship involving more than two entities is called an *n-ary relationship*.

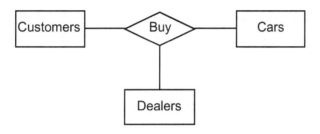

Figure 3.15 N-ary Relationship

Take another example (Figure 3.16) of an employee from a specific department assigned to a certain project. Note that the relationship is diagrammed using Chen notation.

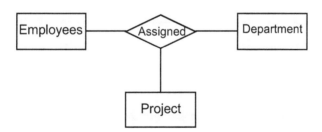

Figure 3.16 N-ary Relationship
Using a Diamond for a Relationship

A straight line can also be used to represent the relationship (Figure 3.17) but those who read a logical data model find the diamond more informative and less confusing.

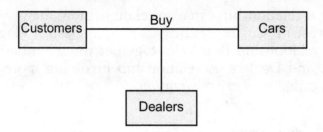

Figure 3.17 N-ary Relationship
Using a Straight Line for a Relationship

Lastly, a relationship might link together multiple occurrences of a single entity type. Take the example of the entity Child and the relationship Sibling. Sibling is used to link together multiple occurrences of Child. When an entity type is related to itself, the *relationship degree* is called *unary* or *recursive* (Figure 3.18).

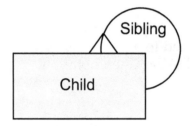

Figure 3.18 Unary Relationship

Another example of a unary relationship is the case where some employees supervise other employees. The relationship Supervises is from Employee to Employee (Figure 4.19).

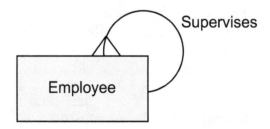

Figure 4.19 A Recursive Relationship

The recursive relationship is also useful for a hierarchy of unknown height. For example, if an organization is divided into a region, district, and section, the modeler can represent it as a three-level structure (Figure 4.20).

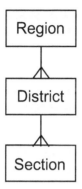

Figure 4.20 A Hierarchical Relationship

However, suppose the number of levels is unknown, or separate locations can be organized differently from one another (e.g., some have districts and others do not). Figure 4.21a no longer accurately represents the organization. However, the recursive relationship can accurately represent an organization of any number of levels (Figure 4.21b).

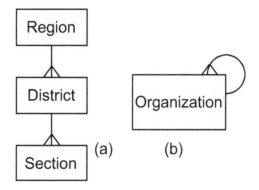

Figure 4.21 (a) A Three-Level Hierarchy,
(b) An N-Level Hierarchy

The recursive relationship is sometimes called a "bill of materials" structure, because it resembles a common parts problem. Imagine an auto parts data model in which a car engine is a part, which includes a starter motor, which is also a part, which includes a solenoid, which is also a part, which includes... Because parts are made up of parts, which are made up of parts, etc., what would the structure look like? Using the recursive relationship, the modeler would create an n-level hierarchy.

All data modeling tools support binary relationships, many support unary relationships, but only a few support n-ary relationships. The reason is a poor one—most database management systems only support binary relationships.

CHAPTER NOTES

[1]Gordon Everest, "Basic Data Structure Models Explained with a Common Example," *Proceedings Fifth Texas Conference on Computing Systems*, IEEE Computer Society, October 18-19 1976, pp. 39-46.

Chapter
4

More About the Entity-Relationship Model

Entia non sunt multiplicands paveter necessitate.
Entities should not be multiplied beyond necessity.
~ Ockham

Good design is like a refrigerator—when it works, no one notices,
but when it doesn't, it sure stinks.
~ Irene Au (designer)

Chapter 2 introduced the simplest type of entity—a *standard, fundamental*, or *proper* entity. However, there are other types of entities, namely *associative entities* and *attributive entities*.

Associative Entities

An *associative entity* is not so much an entity as a relationship that has attributes. Take the entity-relationship pair Customers Buy Cars. MODEL, YEAR, and LIST PRICE are clearly the attributes of Car, while CUSTOMER NAME and CUSTOMER ADDRESS are clearly attributes of Customer. But what about the attributes DATE OF SALE and SALE AMOUNT? They are characteristics of neither the entity Customer nor of the entity Cars but rather of the relationship Buy (Figure 4.1a). When a relationship has attributes, it is called an *associative entity*. An associative entity is represented on the E-R diagram as a boxed diamond—the relationship diamond inside the entity box (Figure 4.1b). The boxed diamond is a fairly universal way to represent an associative entity. Even data modeling tools that do not use a diamond to represent a relationship display the diamond in a box for associative entities.

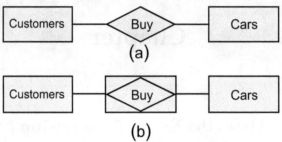

(a)

(b)

Figure 4.1 A Relationship Without (a) and (b) With Attributes

An associative entity can be thought of as either a fundamental entity that is not just *in* a relationship with other entities but *acts* as a relationship with other entities or as a relationship that has its own attributes. Both are correct. Think of it as the Schrodinger's cat of data modeling.

Associative entities can also help make more sense of n-ary relationships. For example, expand the entity-relationship pair, 'Customers Buy Cars' by adding the entity Dealer into the mix, making it 'Customer Buy Cars from Dealers.' Because attributes are properties of an entity, which data object is the attribute PURCHASE DATE a property of? The answer is obviously Buys. Therefore, you have a more realistic situation where:

```
Customer (fundamental entity)
        where CUSTOMER NAME (attribute type)
              is "Howard Johnson" (attribute value)
Buys (associative entity)
        on PURCHASE DATE (attribute type)
              "April 1, 2022" (attribute value)
        for PRICE (attribute type)
              "$1,000" (attribute value)
a Car (fundamental entity)
        MODEL (attribute type)
              "Mustang" (attribute value)
from Dealer (fundamental entity)
        where DEALER NAME (attribute type)
              is "Honest Mike's Used Cars" (attribute value)
```

In this case, Buys must not be a relationship, but rather an associative entity. (Figure 4.2)

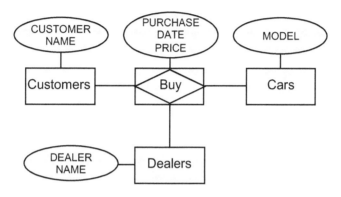

Figure 4.2 Associative Entity Showing Attributes

As with fundamental entities, associative entity attributes can be placed on the E-R diagram or, more popularly, left in the data dictionary.

Attributive (Weak) Entities

A close examination of the Invoice and Line Item entities presented in Chapter 3 should reveal that a Line Item cannot exist without an Invoice. In fact, the very existence of a Line Item depends on the existence of an Invoice. An entity whose existence depends on the existence of another entity is called an *attributive* or *weak entity*. The Line Item entity is dependent on the Invoice entity for its existence, so Line Item is an attributive entity. Some modeling approaches represent an attributive entity with a double box (Figure 4.3). Others use no distinctive graphical symbol.

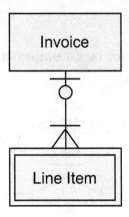

Figure 4.3 An Attributive or Weak Entity

Be careful not to confuse attributive entities with mandatory relationships. One can exist without the other, e.g., it is possible to have a mandatory relationship without entity dependence. Figure 4.4 shows the entity-relationship pair Employee Works In a Factory. Every Employee works in one Factory and every Factory have at least one Employee. Is the relationship mandatory or is one entity existentially dependent on the other?

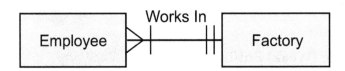

Figure 4.4 A Mandatory Relationship
Without Entity Dependence

The answer is in the definitions of each entity. Because neither the definition of Employee nor Factory relies on the other, both are fundamental entities.

Note that it is also possible for an attributive entity to have an optional relationship. In fact, the attributive entity can be in a mandatory relationship with one entity and in an optional relationship with another. (Figure 4.5a)

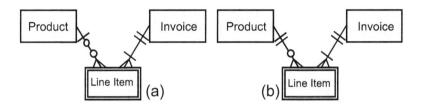

Figure 4.5 An Attributive Entity
(a) With an Optional Relationship and
(b) With Two Mandatory Relationships

Optional existence is *stronger* than entity *weakness*, because entities in an optional relationship with one entity can be in a mandatory relationship with another.

Mandatory relationships can present their own challenges. Figure 4.5b is the same as Figure 4.5a except now Line Item is in a mandatory relationship with both fundamental entities. This raises the question—which entity is Line Item dependent on?

The E-R diagram does not always specify which fundamental entity the attributive entity is dependent on. Here the data dictionary becomes vital. If the definition of the entity is that the entity is dependent on another entity, then it is an attributive entity. However, if the entity does not have such a definition but the relationship does (for example 'Works In' in Figure 4.4), then the relationship is mandatory.

Derived Entities (Phantom Entities)

Derived data can show up as an entity as well as an attribute. A *derived entity*, also called a *phantom entity*, is a set of entity occurrences that is defined by part of another entity's definition, an inaccurate representation of that definition, or a combination of multiple entity definitions. Whereas a derived attribute is the result of a process or formula applied to other attributes, a derived entity is actually a phantom entity that is part of one or more other entities. Most derived entities fall into one of two categories: collections and attributes improperly elevated to entities.

For example, imagine end users insisting that there be yearly or monthly entities to store financial data. They would like to see an entity such as Fiscal Year 2021 or April on the E-R Diagram. The error is collecting financial entity occurrences, that share the same entity definition and placing them into different entity types.

The second derived entity error is very similar. It is taking an attribute, or more technically an attribute value, and creating a different entity for it. For example, take the Customer attribute CUSTOMER STATUS, with the acceptable values "Active" and "Inactive." Some users can be rather adamant that there needs to be one entity named Active Customers and another entity named Inactive Customers.

All derived data—entities and attributes—should be recorded in the data dictionary but not placed on the E-R diagram.

If users find this unacceptable and your best efforts do not dissuade them, then the modeler needs an alternative solution. Luckily, one is presented in Chapter 6.

Supertypes and Subtypes (Also Known as Generalization and Specialization)

Supertypes and *subtypes* are best introduced with an example. Imagine a Customer entity that includes the attributes NAME, ADDRESS, CREDIT STATUS, and CUSTOMER TYPE and the attribute values of CUSTOMER TYPE are either "Retail" or "Wholesale" (Figure 4.6a). However, the Customer entity also includes the attributes DISCOUNT, SALESPERSON, and INDUSTRY CODE (which are only used if the customer is wholesale) and the attributes LOYALTY PROGRAM MEMBER NUMBER, and PROGRAM START DATE (which are only used if the customer is retail). If half the customers are retail and half wholesale, then half of the time the attributes DISCOUNT and LOYALTY PROGRAM MEMBER NUMBER are empty.

Empty data objects make systems developers nervous. If more than one or two attributes are empty, the modeler may suspect something is wrong. To remedy this situation, one could create two entities—Wholesale Customer and Retail Customer (Figure 4.6b); however, this means that certain attributes, such as NAME and ADDRESS, are repeated in the two entities. Duplicate data make some systems developers even more uncomfortable than empty attributes.

(a)   (b)

Figure 4.6 (a) The Customer Entity,
(b) Wholesale and Retail Entities

A second option is to create three entities—Customer, Retail Customer, and Wholesale Customer, where the common attributes are in Customer, retail-specific attributes in Retail Customer, and wholesale-specific attributes in Wholesale Customer (Figure 4.7).

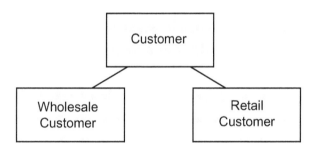

Figure 4.7 Customer, Wholesale, and Retail Entities

The three-entity construct improves on the two-entity construct; however, it still hides important end-user information, namely, that: (1) there is really one entity Customer and not three, and (2) the single object Customer plays two different *roles*—one as a wholesale customer and the other as a retail customer. This more robust view is substantially different from the construct of three separate entities and two relationships.

An improvement on both the two-entity and the three-entity solutions is the supertype/subtype construct. A *subtype* is a *role* an entity plays. The subtype contains the role-specific attributes and relationships. A *supertype* contains the common attributes and the common relationships of all the roles.

In the example, Customer is the supertype containing attributes such as NAME and ADDRESS that are common to all the subtypes. Wholesale and Retail are the subtypes containing the attributes DISCOUNT and LOYALTY PROGRAM MEMBER NUMBER, respectively.

Integral to the notion of supertype/subtype is the concept of *inheritance*. The subtype inherits from the supertype all the supertype's attributes and relationships. The subtype can have its own unique attributes and unique relationships in addition to those it inherits from the supertype.

Supertypes and subtypes are represented any number of ways, although the *box-in-a-box* is a diagrammatic convention popular with many data modelers (Figure 4.8).

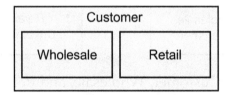

Figure 4.8 Box-in-a-Box Diagramming Convention

The outermost box represents the supertype, and the inner boxes represent the subtypes. There can be as many subtypes boxes as dictated by the organization being modeled (Figure 4.9).

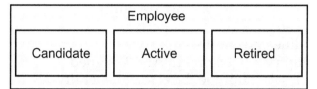

Figure 4.9 Box-in-a-Box Diagramming Convention
with Three Subtypes

Some data modeling books use the terms *generalization* and *specialization* instead of supertype and subtype. *Specialization* is a process for identifying the attributes and relationships in each entity's specific roles. *Generalization* is the process of identifying the attributes and relationships common to all of the entity's roles. Different terminology, same result.

Role-Specific Relationships

Supertype/subtypes are been used to distinguish common attributes found in the supertype from the role-specific attributes found in the subtype. However, supertype/subtypes can also be used to distinguish generic from role-specific relationships.

Expand the Customer example to include the entities Salesperson and Credit History, where all 'Customers Are Assigned a Salesperson,' but only 'Wholesale Customers Have a Credit History.' The box-in-a-box notation can easily represent these generic and role-specific relationships (Figure 4.10).

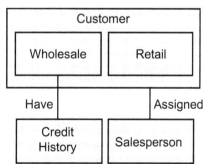

Figure 4.10 Generic and Role-Specific Relationships

Credit History and Salesperson are entities in their own right, so they are placed outside the supertype box. On the diagram the relationship line ends at the supertype Customer box for the entity-relationship pair 'Customers Are Assigned a Salesperson,' and at the Wholesale subtype box for the entity-relationship pair 'Wholesale Customers Have a Credit History.'

Nested Supertypes

There is no reason that a subtype of one supertype cannot be a supertype with its own subtypes. In the Customer example, imagine that there are two different roles for Wholesale Customers, Commercial and Government, each with their own attributes. Figure 4.11 shows a multilevel supertype/subtype graphic for our expanded Customer entity.

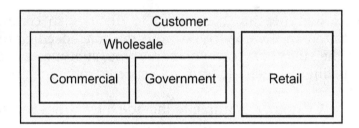

Figure 4.11 Nested Supertypes/Subtypes

Nesting of the supertypes and subtypes can go on for as many levels as necessary.

Reality Hitting Home

Unfortunately, many data modeling tools do not support the box-in-a-box structure—in fact, some do not even support supertypes/supertypes. Alternative methods are required if the data model is to accurately reflect the modeled organization. An alternative solution is the *isa* (is a) construct (Figure 4.12). When using tools that cannot differentiate subtypes and supertypes, modelers can represent subtypes as entities and link the supertype and subtypes in a mandatory relationship so that each subtype occurrence must be linked to a supertype occurrence. The relationship is usually referred to by the clever name of *isa*, which stands for "is a," as in...

Employee *is a* Supervisor
Employee *is a* Retiree
Employee *is a* Trainee

...where Supervisor, Retiree, and Trainee are roles or subtypes of Employee.

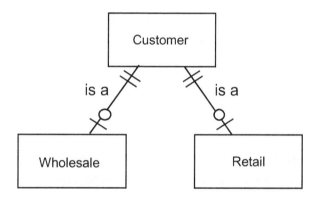

Figure 4.12 Supertype/Subtype Using the *isa* Approach

While it's a good idea, "*isa*-speak" sometimes becomes awkward, as in Customer is a Retail.

As jury-rigged as *isa* might be, sometimes it is the only way to communicate that what appears to be multiple entities and relationships is really a single entity with no relationships and multiple roles.

Note, that even though the subtypes are in an entity box they are not entities but rather the role played by the supertype, and that the *isa* line is not a relationship but simply connects the subtype role with the supertype entity.

While the diagramming tool might not support supertypes and subtypes, the data dictionary must. The textual documentation must tell the complete tale of why three entities and two relationships on the diagram are really one entity, two roles, and zero relationships.

While all of these diagrammatic conventions work, the boxed format has three advantages. It:

- Does not require phantom entities or relationships.

- Can easily accommodate and represent n-level nesting.

- Takes up less space on an often-crowded E-R diagram.

However, later in this chapter, the disadvantages of the box-in-a-box approach become apparent.

Pseudo-Entities and Pseudo-Relationships

Remember, a subtype/subtype structure represents one entity with no relationships. Subtypes are not entities, and the *isa* relationship is not a real relationship. Real relationships are between entities, not roles. Some modelers speak of an *association* between supertypes and subtypes to avoid using the word relationship.

So why is the term relationship used so often to describe a supertype/subtype structure? Many data modeling tools require the use of the data object *relationship* between the subtype and the subtype. The data modeler needs to remember that, when creating a supertype/subtype with these less-than-ideal tools, the subtype entities are pseudo-entities, and the relationships between the supertype and the subtypes are pseud-relationships.

Relationship Constraints: Conjunction, Inclusion, and Exclusion

Relationships are the most complex of the three data modeling objects, so it should be no surprise that they require the most robust concepts to adequately define them. Following are a few additional things every data modeler should know about relationships.

To understand *relationship constraints,* it is useful to go back to your logic course in college. Logic deals with statements that can be either true or false. "John is out" is a simple statement that is either true or false. A compound statement is one made up of two or more simple statements joined together. "John is out *and* he will not be back until tomorrow," is a compound statement consisting of two simple statements: "John is out" (call it simple statement A), and "John will not be back until tomorrow" (call it simple statement B). Determining the truth of compound statements requires an understanding of conjunction and disjunction.

Conjunction states that the compound statement is true if and only if all parts (the simple statements) are true, so "John is out and he will not be back until tomorrow," is only true if simple statement A is true AND simple statement B is true. If either A or B is false, then the compound statement is false. As a quick reference, a conjunction is a compound statement joining two simple statement together using the word *and.*

Disjunction deals with the concept of *or* as in "John is going to town today or tomorrow." This compound statement is true if either simple statement A ("John is going to town today") is true OR if simple statement B ("John is going to town tomorrow") is true. However, disjunction has a wrinkle in it. In a rare display of unity, philosophers, mathematicians, and linguists agree that we really use the word *or* in two very different ways.

Take the statement, "It happened on Tuesday or Wednesday." The compound statement is true if either simple statement A ("It happened on Tuesday") is true OR simple statement B ("It happened on Wednesday") is true. The compound statement is false if neither simple statement is true or if both simple statements are true (because it is an impossibility). This is known as an *exclusive or* and states that a compound statement is true if either A is true OR B is true, but not both.

Moreover, those pesky philosophers, mathematicians, and linguists tell us that there is another and more common use of or—*inclusive or*.

Look at the statement, "Mary will either be a great surgeon *or* a great biologist." If Mary is a great surgeon, then the compound statement is true. It is also true if Mary is a great biologist. Surprisingly or not, it is also true if Mary is a great surgeon and a great biologist. The *or* in the compound statement "Mary will either be a great surgeon *or* a great biologist" is an *inclusive or* meaning that the compound statement is true if simple statement A is true, or if simple statement B is true, or if both simple statements A and B are true. *Inclusive or*, we are told by the experts, is what we normally mean when we use the word *or* in our daily lives.

What does this have to do with data modeling?

A *relationship constraint* is a set of rules that determine how different entity-relationship pairs relate to each other. These rules follow the logical concepts of conjunction, inclusion, and exclusion. Simply substitute *entity* for *simple statement*, *inclusion* for *inclusive or*, *exclusion* for *exclusive or*, *conjunction* for *and*, and one is 90 percent of the way there.

Relationship Constraints: Inclusion

Inclusion is the easiest to understand and the most common. It indicates that entity occurrence A can be related to entity occurrence B, or to entity occurrence C, or to both. Inclusion is the *inclusive or* version of *or*. Figure 4.13 shows the three entities Department, Salaried Employees, and Hourly Employees. An instance of Department could relate to Salaried Employees, or Hourly Employees, or both. Note that inclusion involves not a single relationship, but two separate though interrelated relationships. No special E-R diagramming symbols are required.

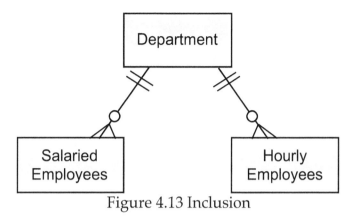

Figure 4.13 Inclusion

Inclusion is, by far, the most common relationship constraint.

Relationship Constraints: Exclusion

Exclusion indicates that an instance of entity A can be related to an instance of entity B or to an instance of entity C, but not both. For example, either a Dealer or a Customer can own a Car, but not both. Exclusion is the *exclusive or* version of *or*. Figure 4.14 uses a curve or arc encompassing the two relationships to represent exclusion.

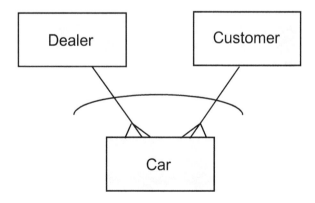

Figure 4.14 Using an Arc to Represent Exclusion

Exclusion is far less common than *inclusion* and often the subject of confusing interactions between data modeling and process modeling.

Many data modeling tools do not graphically represent exclusion, so the only place this information exists is in the data dictionary.

Relationship Constraints: Conjunction

Conjunction is the same as the *and* relationship in logic. It indicates that if A is related to B, it must also be related to C. For example, a business might have a rule stipulating that if a customer has an outstanding balance, then the customer must have a payment plan (Figure. 4.15). Conjunction is diagrammed using a straight line intersecting all of the conjoined relationships.

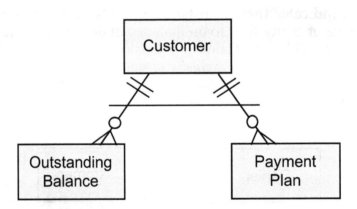

Figure 4.15 Conjunction Showing That Every Customer With an Outstanding Balance Must Have a Payment Plan

As with exclusion, many data modeling tools do not graphically represent conjunction, so the only place this information exists is in the data dictionary.

The three types of relationship constraint are shown in Figure 4.16.

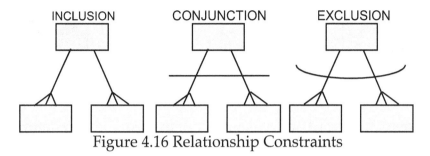

Figure 4.16 Relationship Constraints

You might ask the question: do we really need conjunction? Can't a mandatory relationship do the same thing?

Take the example in Figure 4.15 of the Customer, Outstanding Balance, and Payment Plan entities—if a Customer instance is related to an Outstanding Balance instance, it must also be related to a Payment Plan instance. Note that the relationships between Customer and Outstanding Balance, and Customer and Payment Plan are optional so the concept of conjunction is needed. Why? Because a customer might not have an outstanding balance, so therefore he or she does not need a payment plan. But, if the customer does have an outstanding balance then, and only then, he or she must have a payment plan. Figure 4.17b says that every Customer instance must be related to an Outstanding Balance entity regardless of their payment status—something entirely different from Figure 4.17a. However if the relationships between Customer and Outstanding Balance, and Customer and Payment Plan are mandatory, then, in this case, the conjunction could be diagrammed using only the mandatory relationships. For all practical purposes, IN THIS CASE, conjunction and mandatory relationships are equivalent, and therefore, conjunction is not really needed.

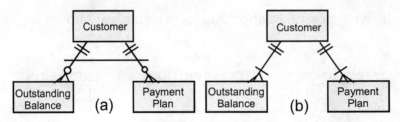

Figure 4.17 Enforcing Relationship Constraints
Using (a) Conjunction and (b) Mandatory Relationships

The operative word above is practical. In theory, a mandatory relationship is a single relationship *between* entities, such as a single
entity-relationship pair, while conjunction encompasses multiple
relationships and multiple entity-relationship pairs.

Now that supertypes/subtypes, relationship constraints, and
membership class have been discussed, we can move on to a case
where the three converge.

Advantages of the *Isa* Structure Over the Box-in-a-Box

In most cases, the box-in-a-box is preferred for graphically representing a supertype/subtype structure. It is compact, easily understandable, and does not confuse the reader with pseudo-
entities or pseudo-relationships. However, there are cases where
the box-in-a-box cannot do the job.

Supertypes and Subtypes and Relationship Constraints

There are a few cases where the *isa* structure better communicates
the nature of the organization.

Case One

Ship Bottom High School, Ship Bottom, NJ uses a super-
type/subtype structure for its Student entity. There is one subtype for Club and another one for Sports (Figure 4.18).

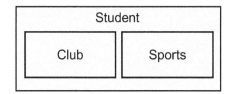

Figure 4.18 School Supertype/Subtype

Alice is in the math club, so Alice's Student entity occurrence includes the Club subtype. Bob is on the track team, so his Student occurrence includes the Sports subtype. Carol is a member of the chess club and the football and wrestling teams, so her Student occurrence includes both the Club and the Sports subtypes.

Case Two

Foggy Bottom High School, Washington D.C. also has a Student supertype/subtype structure. A Student can pick one of two career programs—the academic program, which prepares the student for college (the Academic subtype), or the trade program, which prepares the student for a trade (the Trade subtype) (Figure 4.19).

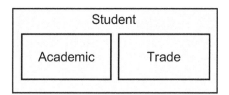

Figure 4.19 School Supertype/Subtype
(a Student Cannot Be in Both Programs)

Hartley is on the academic track, so his Student entity occurrence is associated with the Academic subtype; while Bob, who wants to be an electrician, has his Student entity occurrence associated with the Trade subtype.

Case Three

Hop Bottom High School, Hop Bottom PA also has a Student supertype/subtype structure consisting of a Student supertype; created when the student applies to the school. A Transcript subtype and a Curriculum subtype are created when the student registers for classes (Figure 4.20).

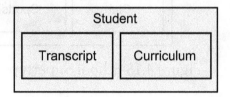

Figure 4.20 School Supertype/Subtype
(Students Must Have Both Subtypes or None of Them)

Sheryl is registered at Hop Bottom High, so her Student occurrence is linked to both the Transcript and Curriculum subtypes.

In Case One (Ship Bottom High School), the supertype/subtype structure is inclusive. A student can be associated with no subtype, or multiple occurrences of one subtype, or both subtypes.

In Case Two (Foggy Bottom High School) the supertype/subtype structure is exclusive. A student can be associated with either subtype, but not both.

In Case Three (Hop Bottom High School) the supertype/subtype structure is a conjunction. A student must be linked to both subtypes or neither.

These are examples of inclusion, exclusion, and conjunction. The question is, how can the modeler represent them using a box-in-a-box? The answer: the modeler can't. However, the modeler can represent this information by using the *isa* structure.

Supertypes and Subtypes, Relationship Constraints, and Membership Class

A supertype can be associated with multiple occurrences of a subtype. Go back to the Ship Bottom High School example with its supertype/subtype structure for its Student entity and its two subtypes for Club and for Sports. Because a student can participate in zero to many clubs and zero to many sports, the supertype/subtype association has a cardinality of one-to-many (Figure 4.21a).

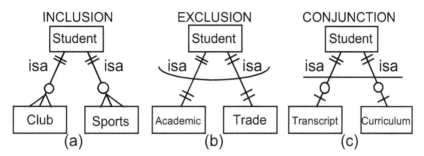

Figure 4.21 Supertype/Subtypes
With (a) Inclusion, (b) Exclusion, and (c) Conjunction

The modality is mandatory-optional because every club and sport needs a student, but a student need not participate in any club or sport. Student is an entity that is not required to have a subtype.

The other two schools also require more information than can be conveyed using the box-in-a-box structure. Foggy Bottom High requires a exclusion constraint on the supertype/subtype structure (Figure 4.21b), while Hop Bottom High requires conjunction (Figure 4.21c).

Note the association of the subtype to the supertype is always mandatory.

The *isa* is the only structure that allows the modeler to display the supertype/subtypes membership class as well as its relationship constraints.

A Better Way to Diagram Supertypes and Subtypes

There are two reasons there are so many ways to represent supertypes and subtypes. The first is that Chen never included them in his original work. Other authors stepped into the fray with various ways of filling the void. The second reason is that it is difficult to represent the complexity of the concept while making it diagrammatically simple and informative.

This book presents the two most popular options for displaying supertypes. The first option, the box-in-a-box, is the easiest to understand but the least information rich. The second option, called *isa*, that stands for "is a," is the richest in conveying information but can lead to some confusion, not to mention having to use the term, "isa."

Problems Arise

There are two problems with both the box-in-a-box and *isa*. First, they both use a rectangle to graphically display a subtype. However, a subtype is not an entity but rather a role an entity plays. Using the same symbol for both entities and roles is not only confusing but can convey the wrong message to the diagram reader—that there are multiple entities when there is really only one.

Second, the *isa* structure uses a line to represent the association between the supertype and its subtypes—the same graphical symbol that is used to represent a relationship between entities. Again, this can be confusing and send the wrong message to the diagram reader—that there is a relationship when, in fact, there is none.

And Now for Something Completely Different—A Modest Proposal

There is a third option for graphically displaying supertypes—one that is unique to this book:

•   Represent the subtype with a rounded-corner rectangle.

•   Use a dashed line to represent the role between the supertype and the subtype.

Both features are displayed in Figure 4.22.

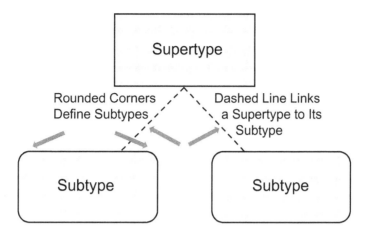

Figure 4.22 Option 3 For Representing
Supertypes and Subtypes

Option 3 has two advantages over Option 1, the box-and-a-box, and Option 2, the *isa* construct. First, Option 3 uses a rounded-cornered rectangle for a subtype, so subtypes no longer look the same as entities. Second, the role that connects the supertype and the subtype is a dashed line, not a solid one. When using Option 3, there should be no confusion between an entity and a subtype or between a relationship and a role.

However, Option 3 also has two disadvantages. First, a rectangle with rounded corners and the dashed line are used, with various meanings, by other data modeling approaches, such as IDEF1X and UML.

Second, Option 3 runs the risk, as do many compromises, of pleasing nobody. It was not published in some scholarly journal or accredited by some standards organization. It is, shall we say, homegrown. It raises the very real question; do we really need another graphical symbol?

THE END OF THE BEGINNING (to quote Winston Churchill)

You should now have a complete beginner's view of the logical data model. Figure 4.23 should be helpful in keeping things straight. The next chapter delves into the tasks required to actually construct a logical data model.

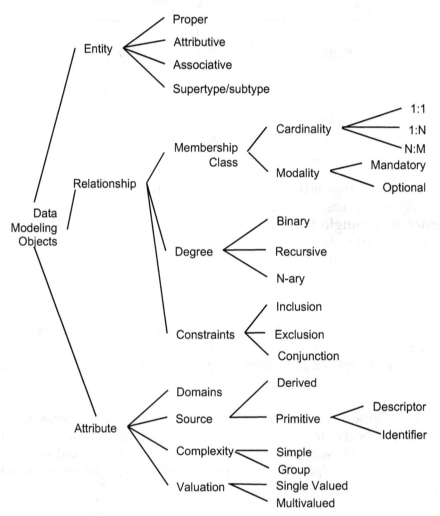

Figure 4.23 The Logical Data Modeling Family Tree

Chapter
5

Building the Logical Data Model

The single biggest problem in communication is the illusion that it has taken place.
~ George Bernard Shaw

Still, this whole grim reaper thing should have come with a manual.
Or a diagram of some kind. A flowchart would have been nice.
~ Darynda Jones (author)

Truth is, building a logical data model is a rather simple task. Just follow the steps presented in this chapter, and you have a data model. Although the process is simple, it is not easy. The modeler must interact with other people to data model, and people complicate things. Granted, everyone might have a common goal, but that neither implies a common agenda nor a common path to that goal. And, contrary to what the pundits profess, getting there is often *not* half the fun.

However, this does not mean that all is hopeless. There are steps you can take to ease the transition from here to there. What follows lays the foundation for building, verifying, and maintaining a logical data model—without going crazy.

Getting Started

Logical data modeling is not just an exercise for technical staff. To be effective, users must be fully involved, and that involvement should begin as early in the effort as possible. Data modeling is an iterative process that has a starting point followed by an almost endless procession of refinements before the end is reached.

The model is chiseled, crafted, and enhanced until it honestly and effectively represents the subject. Figure 5.1 shows both the simplicity and repetitiveness of the task. There are three simple steps: (1) gather information and review, (2) analyze information, and (3) construct model.

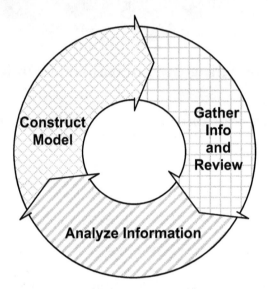

Figure 5.1 The Logical Data Modeling Lifecycle

At its simplest level, logical data modeling is a series of rather unimposing steps.

Step 1: Gather Information and Review

1.1   Gather and review existing system information. Documents can include technical specifications for the existing system and user manuals for business staff.

1.2   Identify people who are experts or experienced in the subject. This can include both technical staff and business staff from senior managers to clerks.

1.3   Meet with these experts and uncover the "things" (entities) the subject (application) is about and how they relate to each other. Start simple, identifying the top 10 entities, then expand to identify relationships and attributes.

Step 2: Analyze Information

2.1   Identify the data objects (entities, attributes, and relationships) in the documentation found in Step 1.

2.2.   Merge the data objects revealed from the documentation with those unearthed from staff interviews.

2.3   Uncover missing information and inconsistencies from the analysis of the documents and interviews. Identify new questions to ask experts.

Step 3: Construct Model

3.1   Graph the entities and relationships using the graphical conventions described in Chapters 2, 3, and 4.

3.2   Define, in detail, the data objects, and enter the information into the data dictionary.

3.3   Create the documentation and presentations needed to walk subject experts through the progress of the model.

Repeat Step 1: Gather Information and Review

1.1   Review, one at a time, each data object with technical and business staff, expanding and/or modifying the logical data model as necessary, with new entities, relationships, and attributes. Gather and review newly identified systems information.

1.2   Identify additional people who are experts or experienced in the subject who should be interviewed.

1.3   Meet with these new experts and review, one at a time, each data object with technical and business staff, expanding and/or modifying the logical data model, as necessary, with new entities, relationships, and attributes.

Repeat Step 2: Analyze Information

Repeat Step 3: Construct Model

Repeat Steps 1, 2, and 3 as often as necessary until there is an overwhelming consensus that the process is complete.

Data modeling can begin as early as the project planning phase (to help estimate project costs and schedules), or it can wait until project kickoff. In addition, it can be performed one on one or in a group setting.

The logical data modeler has four sources of information: (1) the people who commissioned the new system, (2) the people who use or support the existing system and/or will use the new system, (3) the documentation about the existing system, and finally (4) the actual innards of the existing system. This book focuses on 1 and 2 and the techniques to facilitate interviewing these sources. Sources 3 and 4 should be all too familiar to systems developers, so they are not discussed here.

As the first step, identify who should be consulted to understand the subject. The list can include user and technical staff and extend from senior management to junior clerks. You should be selective in choosing interviewees to ensure that they represent all aspects of the organization—include both those who are knowledgeable about the way things *are done* and those who know the way they *should be done*. This last point is important. All too often, a new system merely offers a faster, cheaper way of doing things the same way they have always been done when what really is needed is a new way of doing things. So, talk to both the historian and the visionary, but remember which is which.

Because the interview list will likely include both user and technical staff, you might expect to encounter differences in their reaction to application development techniques such as data modeling. Surprisingly, their responses are amazingly similar—some will be open to data modeling techniques, while others will be indifferent or even hostile to them.

Oddly enough, the hostility sometimes comes more from the technical rather than the user side. While some may genuinely question the validity or payback of using data modeling techniques, others feel threatened by them. New ways of doing things represent change, and change is often the most difficult thing for people to accept. The successful data modeler needs to recognize and negotiate these hurdles.

No doubt, some people are selected for interviews because they are too important or noisy to ignore. In this case, you should go through all the proper steps, but in the end, use your judgment to decide what should be in the model and what should be excluded.

> It is a good idea for the logical data modeling team (even if it is a team of one) to have a champion to pave the way and facilitate the process. A champion is a sufficiently senior member of the technical or business staff who has an interest in the successful completion of the project, will stand up for the team, and, because of his or her status, will be listened to by participants. Champions are common at the project manager level, although there is no reason why they cannot exist at the logical data modeling level as well.

Although a certain amount of data can be gained from documents, most information is gathered from personal interviews (if nothing else, the interviews can identify what documents exist and which should be read). The two approaches for collecting data through interviews are the *informal one-on-one interview* and *facilitated joint session* involving a number of participants.

Informal One-on-One Interviews

The most popular way to gather data modeling information is the *one-on-one interview*, which involves sitting down with an interviewee and asking questions about the subject. An interview session can range from 30 minutes to 2 hours and involve a number of short return visits to resolve questions, confusions, and issues. A good way to get started is to ask the interviewee to name the 10 basic "things" in which the organization is involved. Some of the things mentioned might be outside the scope of the project—use them to gain agreement on what is in and what is out of scope.

This helps set the boundaries of the interview and reaffirms the core mission of the project.

Examples are useful. Start by suggesting common entities such as customers, accounts, or employees. When approximately 10 entities have been identified, ask about the relationships among them, e.g., "Can a customer have more than one account?"

Some interviewees are able to expound on their data; however most must be prompted. (User soliloquies are more likely to occur during process modeling interviews where known sequences of steps or events exist; they are rare in data modeling.) Be prepared to take the lead with a series of easily answered questions.

The information you collect can be either written down in long hand or diagrammed on the spot, whichever method is easier for you. New data modelers might not feel comfortable extemporaneously drawing diagrams; even so, if diagramming on the fly is possible, then do so because (as explained with the genealogy example in Chapter 1) diagrams make it easier to identify problems and omissions. They also can function as the trigger for new questions.

Some interviewers like a scribe—another logical data modeler—to join the interview to diagram what is uncovered. However, be cautious. Too many people in the room can sometimes intimidate or overwhelm the interviewee and effectively shut down the meeting.

Expect follow-up interviews to confirm what was heard in the previous session, answer additional questions, and/or gain additional information.

Facilitated Joint Session

Not all interviews are one on one. Group interviews are a time-saving alternative to meeting with one person at a time. The *facilitated joint session* is a gathering or workshop of a number of users together, along with a logical data modeler as a facilitator, to build a complete logical data model. The goal is to get the attendees talking, back and forth, primarily among themselves, with help from the facilitator.

A facilitated joint session:

- Is usually a single session that can last from 1 to 3 days.
- Consists of 4 to 10 participants.
- Follows a formal set of rules.
- Is led by a facilitator who orchestrates and adjudicates the discussions.
- Rarely requires follow-up sessions.

The goal of the session is to derive a complete data model in the time allotted. The rules stipulate that everybody is to be present for the entire session, that all are heard, and that neither a single individual nor a single issue dominates the meeting. The result of the session should be a model that all agree represents the organization.

Joint sessions can gather information quickly; however, they require more preparation by the data modeler. The facilitator should either have a scribe present (another logical data modeler) who records all that is said and diagrams the information on the fly on a white board, or the facilitator needs to do these tasks. Follow-up meetings are rare, so the single session needs to be comprehensive. However, if questions do arise and additional user input is needed, you can always contact individual participants for additional information.

Theoretically, participants can be executives down to clerks. The joint session rules state that during the session, all are equal with equal rights to be heard and to object. "Rank left at the door" is an often sited motto. However, reality is sometimes not so codified. Regardless of any rules, junior staff are often shy about speaking out in front of senior managers much less disagreeing with them. Luckily, for the data modeler, the question is often moot because executives tend to prefer one-on-one interviews befitting their status or schedules.

Whether you are interviewing senior managers or holding sessions with junior staff, you must be prepared. The best way to be prepared is to gather and review every scrap of information available about the current system, the proposed system, manuals created for end users, or IT documentation—in fact, any piece of paper dealing with the subject that you can find. Being prepared makes the interviews or sessions go more quickly, results in more accurate information, and annoys the participants less. Participants sometimes show little patience for the unprepared.

Unpacking a Statement

Converting interviewee ramblings to data modeling input is a bit of an art because it involves translating English to an E-R diagram. Chapters 3 and 4 explained that, "Customers can have more than one account, but an account can be for one and only one customer," could be easily transferred to an E-R diagram (Figure 5.2) by converting English text to data modeling objects. *Customers* and *accounts* become entities, *have* becomes the relationship *Owns*, while the language "one and only one" becomes the cardinality and modality of the relationship.

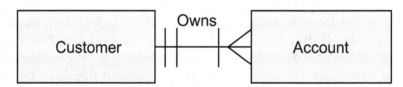

Figure 5.2 An E-R Diagram Expresses English Statements

Table 5.1 is a chart that is helpful when translating English into data modeling-ese. (A more detailed account of converting English syntax to data modeling constructs can be found in Peter Chen's excellent papers on the subject.[1]) To use the chart, look up the English part of speech or the words used in the English statement on the left side of the chart and read the data-modeling construct on the right.

Table 5.1 English to E-R Conversion Chart

WHAT TO LOOK FOR	E-R COMPONENT
Common Noun	Proper Entity Type
Proper Noun	Proper Entity Instance
Transitive Verb	Relationship
Intransitive Verb	Attribute
Gerund	Associative Entity
Adjective	Proper Entity Attribute
Adverb	Relationship Attribute (Associative Entity)
Words such as: "many" "at least" "one" "only one" "at most"	Cardinality
Words such as: "must" "can" "may not"	Modality
Words such as: "and" "but"	Conjunction
Words such as: "or" "either...or" "nor" "neither...nor"	Exclusion

Take the following example:

"Employees can report to either a supervisor or the personnel department."

- Employee and Supervisor are common nouns and, there-fore, entities.

- Personnel Department is a proper noun, not a common noun (such as organization or department), so the modeler should create an entity called Organization with an occurrence containing the attribute value, "Personnel Department."

- Report is a verb and, therefore, a relationship.

- Exclusion is implied by the words "either...or."

- "Can" indicates that the relationship is optional, but that is already known from the exclusion construct.

- The plural of employees and the singular form for supervisor and organization says the cardinality is one to many.

What the statement does not indicate, however, is the complete modality of the relationship (e.g., must a supervisor have at least one report?). Nor does it indicate whether supervisor should be an entity or a role (subtype) of Employee (Figure 5.3). These issues must be probed by the interviewer.

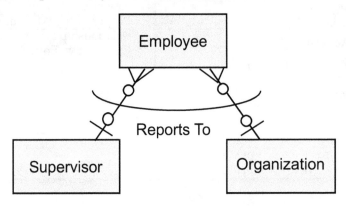

Figure 5.3 E-R Diagram for
"Employees can report to either a supervisor
or personnel department."

Take a second example: "Orders are shipped from the warehouse promptly."

- Orders and warehouse are common nouns and, therefore, entities.

- Shipped is the verb and, therefore, the relationship.

- "Promptly" is an adverb, so it is a relationship attribute. (Actually, it represents two attributes—ORDER DATE and SHIPPING DATE—which means that "shipped" is really an associative entity (Figure 5.4).)

Figure 5.4 E-R Diagram for
"Orders are shipped from the warehouse promptly."

Some statements are more difficult, and neither the English to E-R diagramming technique, in particular, nor data modeling, in general, can accurately represent them. For example: "An employee cannot report to his or her spouse."

Employee is an entity and *reports* is a relationship. What might not be so obvious is the second relationship implied by the word spouse. The diagram might look something like that in Figure 5.5. What one cannot capture in the diagram is the fact that if the nature of the family relationship between two employees is spouse, then one cannot report to the other. That information exists only in the data dictionary.

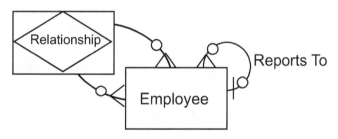

Figure 5.5 E-R Diagram for
"An employee cannot report to his or her spouse."

There is an important lesson in this example. If data modeling models data, and process modeling models processes, which technique models rules? Actually, and unfortunately, the answer is both. Rules such as "Every employee is assigned to one, and only one, department" are easily modeled by E-R techniques. However, that an employee cannot report to his or her spouse cannot be modeled by current data modeling techniques alone. Process modeling must also be used to represent rules.

It would be nice if there were some rule-modeling technique that could be used to review all organization rules; however, for now at least, to understand the rules of the organization, you must rely on both the data and process models.

This underscores one important lesson. Regardless of the techniques or tools used (data modeling, process modeling, flow chats, etc.), there are times where good old-fashioned text cannot be beat. And, where should this good old-fashioned text exist? Well, in the data dictionary, the repository of the most detailed information about data and processes.

The Two Data Modeling Components

So far, emphasis has been on how data objects are represented on an E-R diagram, but this is only part of the story. In fact, a data model is both a graphical representation depicting the system's data objects (the E-R diagram) and also a repository of information about the data an organization uses or needs (the data dictionary).

Look upon a data model as consisting of two separate components:

•   Presentation component, consisting of the Entity-Relationship diagram.

•   Documentation component, consisting of the data dictionary.

The documentation component contains all the data you need to create the presentation component; however, not everything in the data dictionary is on the E-R diagram. For example, as mentioned in Chapter 2, derived data (such as the totals that appear on a report) are not included on the E-R diagram because they are more of a process than static data (see the Chapter 8 section on Derived Data). However, derived data are still important, that is why they are in the data dictionary—just not on the E-R diagram.

Also, be wary of derived data posing, not as an attribute, but as an entity. Some end users, even some data modelers, struggle with the subset of an entity appearing as a separate entity or attributes incorrectly assumed to be an entity. Look to the entity and attribute definitions in the data dictionary to uncover what are legitimate parts of the E-R diagram and what are not.

Information Required for Data Modeling

The data modeling process collects detailed information about each of the identified data objects. As noted below, the information should include, but not necessarily be limited to, complete definitions of entities, relationships, and attributes such as:

1. Entities
    a. Name
    b. Definition
    c. Entity type (proper, associative, attributive)
    d. Synonyms or aliases
        (other user names for this entity)
    e. Attributes in the entity
        (1) Name
        (2) Percent of time attribute value occurs
    f. Roles the entity plays (subtypes)
    g. Number of occurrences of the entity
    h. Growth rate
    i. Insertion, update, deletion rules
    j. Notes, rules, and comments

2. Relationships
    a. Name
    b. Definition
    c. Entities in the relationship
    d. Attributes in the relationship
        (1) Name
        (2) Percent of time attribute value occurs
    e. Membership class (cardinality, modality)
    f. Degree (unary, binary, n-ary)
    g. Constraints (conjunction, inclusion, exclusion)
    h. Notes, rules, and comments

3.   Attributes
        a.   Name
        b.   Definition
        c.   Synonyms or aliases
                (names from other users or applications)
        d.   Source (primitive or derived, descriptor or identifier
                (for identifiers: compound or concatenated))
        e.   Complexity (simple (participation in group)
                or group (attributes in group))
        f.   Valuation (single valued or multivalued)
        g.   Domain
        h.   Format and size
        i.   Notes, rules, and comments

4.   Domains
        a.   Name
        b.   Definition
        c.   Format
        d.   Synonyms or aliases (other names for this domain)
        e.   Participation in other domains
        f.   Default values
        g.   Acceptable values
        h.   Notes, rules, and comments

Note that domains have their own area in the dictionary. The reason is simple; usually only a few domains help define many attributes. It is easier to describe the domains once and then simply reference them in the attribute definitions. It also makes it easier to identify attributes that share the same domain—important information for process modelers and database schema designers.

Not all CASE or data modeling tools have dictionaries that can store all of this information. In such cases, you must find some other documentation method. One acceptable solution is to include the information in the data object comments field that is found in most tools. It is a good idea to develop a convention for identifying these special cases. To signal a special field within the comments area, for example, use the programming concept of *reserve words,* spelled in all uppercase, as in:

```
DOMAIN = Dates between 1/1/50 and 12/31/99
ATTRIBUTE COMPLEXITY = simple
```

In this example, the all uppercase denotes the reserved words *domain* and *attribute complexity* and that the text following the reserved words indicates that, in the first case, the domain of the attribute is a range between two dates and in the second case that the attribute complexity is *simple.*

Verifying the Model

It is rare for anyone, doing anything, to do it right the first time. The data model is no exception and must be verified multiple times during development. There are two common methods of verification, immediate *interview feedback* and *formal walkthroughs.*

Interview Feedback

The best time to correct mistakes and omissions is during the interview process. Constantly read back to the interviewee what you heard. This not only ensures that the interviewee is understood but also gives the interviewee an opportunity to correct what was said.

Most non-technical staff underreport business rules and constraints. You might need to push them to uncover the boundaries of entities and relationships. For example, if told that, "every account is owned by a customer," then you should follow up and ask whether firm, transient, suspense, or general ledger accounts exist. If you are told that there is only one customer for an account, you should ask whether multiple family members could use the same account. You must probe to test the limits of what the interviewee reports.

You also must reassess the entire revised model after adding new interviewee information. Does the new information add to the clarity of the model or does it create new questions? Is the information gathered from interviewees inconsistent with other sources? You should confirm that the revisions make sense, apply them to the model, and then go back to some, or all, of those interviewed to show them a draft of the revised model and solicit additional comments, corrections, and additions.

How many times the model needs to be verified by users depends on whether new useful information is being gained or not.

Formal Walkthrough

In contrast to interview feedback, the *formal walkthrough* generally takes place sometime after the completion of the interviews or the joint session. The walkthrough usually includes four to eight of the interviewees or joint-session participants. More preparation is needed for the walkthrough than for interview feedback, such as overhead projection of the model, individual copies of the model and data dictionary, prepared questions, etc. Distributing the model a day or two before the session is sometimes helpful.

Regardless of whether you use interview feedback, a formal walkthrough, or both, to many interviewees, data modeling looks more confusing and less appealing than multiplying roman numerals (Figure 5.6). The successful modeler needs to *walk* or guide the users through the model, applying a high level of patience.

There are three ways to walk users through the data model: (1) escort the interviewee through the E-R diagram slowly and confirm each data item, (2) convert the model back into English and read the model aloud in a narrative style, or (3) do both.

With some interviewees, you can simply draw the model on paper or a white board during the initial interview or, alternatively, unveil the printed model during the formal walkthrough. If you describe what is being done, line-by-line, many people are able to follow the analysis sufficiently to point out errors and omissions. Other people are more comfortable being read to. In that case, you should be prepared to interpret the data model to them in English.

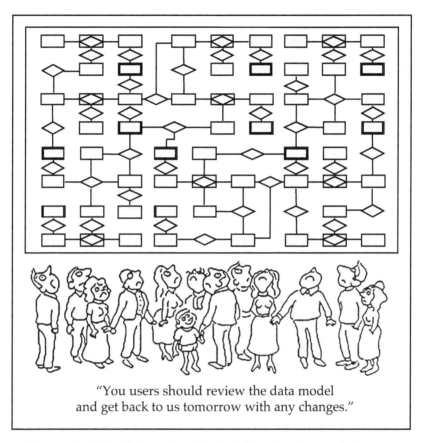

"You users should review the data model
and get back to us tomorrow with any changes."

Figure 5.6 Verifying the Model Can Be Overwhelming

Which method is chosen depends on the receptivity of the inter-viewee to data modeling jargon, although using both methods is probably the surest way of developing a useful data model. In either case, keep the conversation on a user level. There is no bet-ter way to stop a promising interview or walkthrough than to get into techno-babble. Talk about user data, user activities, and user relationships.

Data Model Acceptance

A constantly changing data model is not useful input to physical database design. At some point, the modeling process needs to shift from development to maintenance. Acceptance (by business-user representatives and IT) indicates that the model accurately reflects the organization at a point in time and that subsequent changes should be handled through a change control process.

Acceptance is an official process involving a representative of the business organization formally recognizing that the data model is accurate, complete, and adequate, and a representative of IT proclaiming the model meets all IT standards. It is one of the development milestones for application development.

In practice, many users are reluctant to sign off on anything that doesn't produce something user tangible, such as a functioning system. If the signoff is specifically stated in the project plan, then there should be little difficulty, although user management might seek some outside confirmation. If the project plan did not specify an official signoff, or if the plan is fuzzy on the subject, then you need to explain what the user is getting into by signing off and what he or she is getting into by *not* signing off. If it is clearly explained that signoff is a critical step for completing the system, compliance usually prevails.

Maintaining the Model

Clearly, tools and techniques are helpful in building a data model, but they are not always enough for maintaining it. Imagine the following problem:

> A banking application is being built using an iterative development approach. As it moves into integration, the team discovers that while an account belongs to a customer, a customer can relate to another "customer," and although this "other customer" does not have an account, the bank must save information about that customer as well. For example, the bank might have accounts for Thomas Rowley Real Estate Inc. and Thomas Rowley Travel Services Inc., but no account for the parent company, Thomas Rowley Holding Company. Unfortunately, available credit information is kept on the holding company level, not the subsidiaries.

Because of the change, the designers modified the database design to allow:

- Customers to be related to other customers.
- Customers who are not related to any accounts.

To keep the documentation complete and accurate, someone must go back to the data model created earlier and update it to reflect these two changes.

Oddly enough, many organizations do not have a mechanism to accommodate maintaining a previously built data model. Frequently, data modelers are not informed about changes to the organization or to the application that have data model implications. Moreover, the project data modeling team might have been disbanded once the original model was completed. Nevertheless, if documentation is to be complete and accurate, and it must be if maintenance is to be hassle free, a mechanism is needed to ensure that the data model remains consistent with the application.

Some tools can help alleviate this problem. Data modeling reengineering tools, for example, can read a database schema and generate the data model from it. These tools could ease some of the maintenance hassle.

CHAPTER NOTES

[1]Peter Chen, "English Sentence Structure and Entity-Relationship Diagrams," *Information Sciences*, 29, 2-3, 1983, pp. 127-149.
and
Peter Chen, "English, Chinese, and ER Diagrams," *Data & Knowledge Engineering*, Vol. 23, No. 1, June 1997, pp. 5-16.

Chapter
6

Some Useful Techniques and Tips
for Building a Logical Data Model

There will come a time when you believe everything is finished.
That will be the beginning.
~ Louis L'Amour

Fools you are...who say you like to learn from your mistakes...
I prefer to learn from the mistakes of others, and avoid the cost of my own.
~ Otto von Bismarck

Data modeling tools have become an important component of systems development but they have not changed the fundamentals of logical data modeling. The thought processes and interpersonal skills that were required before tools existed are still needed now. However, tools do allow the use of new views of the data that can facilitate user understanding. Three new and useful advances are *subject area, neighborhood,* and *entity fragment diagrams.*

Subject Area Diagrams

If you are modeling a school project or writing a book on data modeling, then the E-R diagram is relatively simple. Rarely will the student or reader encounter a diagram with more than 10 entities. However, the real world of data modeling is quite different. Models of 100 entities are not unheard of. Because models of this size can scare the modeler, imagine what they can do to the user who is expected to help verify them. The best solution for managing such a leviathan is to make large imposing diagrams smaller friendlier ones. The subject area diagram is one technique for achieving modeling harmony.

A *subject area diagram* is a subset of a data model consisting of only subject-related entities and relationships. For example, the data model for a savings bank might include customer, account, and product subject areas, each containing a number of related entities. A manufacturer might have one subject area for sourcing, one for assembly, and a third for distribution.

Subject areas can serve a number of different purposes. First, a subject area can function as a limited depiction of an organization's data (Figure 6.1), presenting the user with a less intimidating diagram.

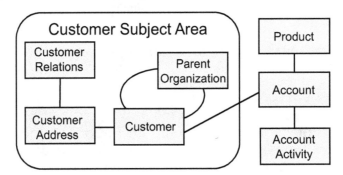

Figure 6.1 Customer Subject Area Diagram

Second, a subject area can help limit the scope of a data-modeling interview. Referring to the above example, an interview could be limited to just the customer-related entities.

Third, a subject area can be the basis for dividing the data modeling workload among staff. If three teams are developing the data model, assigning a separate subject area to each team reduces the interaction that must go on among teams.

The result is an entity grouping or clustering based on commonality of definition.

Subject areas are not a fundamental part of a data model but one of a number of tools to aid the data modeler or developers in creating, understanding, and using the data model. They do not re-place the E-R diagram. Rather the subject area is a temporary snapshot or view of a piece of the model. It rarely exists after the project is complete.

Neighborhood Diagrams

A real-world data model can be an imposing diagram. However, a number of data modeling tools allow the production of a *neighborhood diagram*, which shows one entity at a time with only its relationships and the entities that are tied to those relationships. If the data model contains 50 entities, then there are 50 neighborhood diagrams.

Neighborhood diagrams can be particularly helpful when conducting follow-up interviews because only those entities relevant to the interviewee need be displayed. With neighborhood diagrams, many users, in particular, those who do not need to see the complete data model, can review a graphical subset of their data without becoming overwhelmed (Figure 6.2).

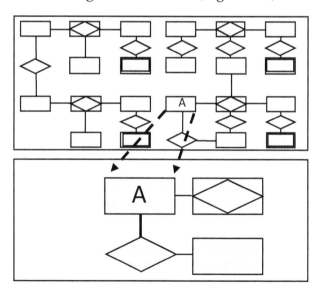

Figure 6.2 Neighborhood Diagram for Entity A

As with subject areas, neighborhood diagrams are ephemeral, existing only as views of the complete data model. Once they have served their purpose, they are best discarded and created anew if they are ever needed again.

Entity Fragment Diagrams

An *entity fragment diagram* is a view or portion of the data model that deals with a specific process or function and is most useful for process modelers and the business users they interview. Take the example of the "Update Customer Account" function created during process modeling. This process might need Customer, Account, and Credit data but might not be concerned with the Production Schedule, Raw Materials, or Distributors entities. Some tools allow modelers to create a subset of the data model specifying only the entities, attributes, and relationships relevant for a specific process (Figure 6.3).

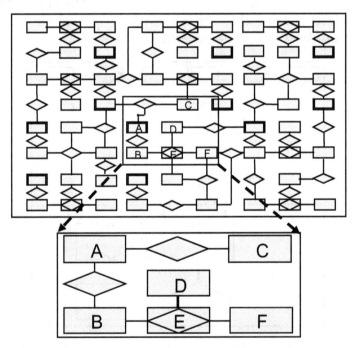

Figure 6.3 Entity Fragment Diagram

When reviewing the process, the entity fragment diagram displays only process-relevant data.

Entity fragment diagrams are useful for explaining to users the connection between process and data. They are even more useful for technical staff charged with creating project process models, system designs, and application code. Some database schema designers review them when creating database views and subschemas.

Although the entity fragment diagram might be a process model tool, its creation is often the domain of the logical data modeler.

Relationship Bridges and Stubs

Real-world logical data models can become cluttered. As the number of entities and relationships increases, the chances that a relationship line will cross another relationship line also increases (Figure 6.4). As the number of crossed lines increases, the communications value of the diagram decreases. Eventually, as the diagram starts to look like a plate of linguine, the diagram becomes incomprehensible.

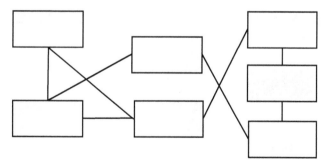

Figure 6.4 Crossed Relationship Lines

You can imagine therapist offices filled with logical data modelers driven to the edge by having to move boxes around on a diagram trying to uncross crossed relationship lines, only to discover that after resolving one crossed line, three more pop up—a sort of data modeling whack-a-mole. Their mental health is jeopardized in the futile quest to find the holy grail of data modeling—an entire diagram without any crossed relationship lines.

First, logical data modelers should know that a crossed line or two is not the end of the world. The relationship incursions can be easily explained away at meetings and with notes or warnings attached to the diagram (see the Clouds section in this chapter). More than a few crossed lines, however, become problematic. Luckily, the data modeling pioneers from the corporate systems development trenches have a solution or two.

Second, if there are only a few crossed lines, and the entities in the crossed relationships are close together on the diagram, then the data modeler can insert *bridges*, little crossovers, to show that the lines are not connected (Figure 6.5). Experience shows that users have little trouble understanding what the bridges mean.

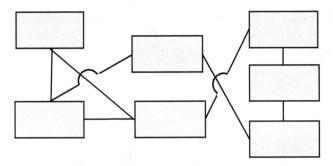

Figure 6.5 Using Bridges to Resolve
Crossed Relationship Lines

Third, if there are a large number of crossovers, or if the entities in the relationship are not close together on the diagram, then the modeler can insert relationship *stubs*—small lettered circles—that link together two parts of a relationship line (Figure 6.6). Stubs work equally well whether the entities in the relationship are next to each other or on opposite sides of the diagram.

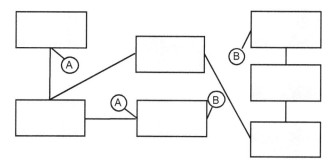

Figure 6.6 Using Stubs to Resolve Crossed Relationship Lines

Whether relationship lines are crossed or not and whether bridges or stubs are used, the principle is the same—The Third Logical Design Principle: Communication. The data modeler must do what is necessary to fulfill a primary mission of the model and that is to communicate to users and systems designers alike the true nature of the organization's data.

The Two Logical Data Diagrams

One of the dilemmas the data modeler faces relates to size and complexity. A complete logical data model can have more than 100 entities and relationships and many hundreds of attributes. Add to that attributive and associative entities, super-types/subtypes, and recursive relationships, and the result is a complex E-R diagram suitable for wallpapering a large room. Such real-world models can be too complex, technical, and confusing for many users. Users often require a simpler diagram, with fewer hieroglyphics, that represents data concepts that are more meaningful to them. Subject area, neighborhood, and entity fragment diagrams help, but they only display a piece of the model. Sometimes, users need a diagram that displays the scope of the entire model, but at a higher level. On the other hand, systems analysts and physical designers need detailed information about the data the organization or application uses. Their needs argue for a complete and exacting diagram.

The solution is actually quite easy. Create two diagrams, both expressing the same data, but at two different levels of detail. The two E-R diagrams are the *end-user diagram* and the *detailed diagram.*

- The end-user diagram:

  — Presents an end-user-oriented view.
  — Reflects a high-level interpretation of the data.
  — Includes only the basic entities and relationships with examples of attributes.
  — Is often at the organization level.

- The detailed diagram:

  — Represents a systems and business analyst view.
  — Provides a detailed level of information.
  — Gives information about all entities, relationships, and some attributes.
  — Is application oriented.

Timing and focus differentiate the two diagrams. The end-user diagram is often created during the earlier stages of the development cycle. This is possible because the end-user diagram requires less analysis than the detailed diagram. However, both diagrams require constant refinement during the development process (Figure 6.7).

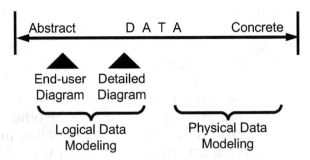

Figure 6.7 The End-User and Detailed Diagrams

The end-user diagram might be created and needed during the planning stage to support project cost and schedule estimates. Attributes associated with the end-user diagram are representative or examples. Modelers sometimes use the phrase "such as" to indicate that the entity contains information *such as* account type or tax classification. Exact attribute identification is part of the complete logical data model.

The detailed diagram excludes derived data, has numerous subtypes, and expresses all relationships between entities. On the other hand, the end-user diagram might only show major fundamental entities and significant relationships and might include derived entities such as Position and Customer Balance, if they have significant meaning for users. Nonetheless, the detailed diagram is *the* E-R diagram from which all explanatory aids, such as subject area diagrams, neighborhood diagrams, and the end-user diagram, are derived.

Even though the end-user diagram is a preliminary or first-cut diagram, it should not always be discarded after development of the detailed diagram. For many end users, the end-user diagram is a more comfortable representation of the business with which they are familiar. It is sometimes a good idea to keep the end-user diagram up to date for use in user presentations and documentation.

Remember, the emphasis is on communication (the third logical design principle). The information needs of the physical designers are very different from the information users require. Whereas the detailed diagram is necessary to build an application system, the end-user diagram can be an important option if it contributes to user understanding of the project. Typically, the decision to produce only the detailed diagram or to produce both is left to the individual project team. Both diagrams exist in popular methodologies.

Having two diagrams is not as difficult as it might seem. First, the end-user diagram might already be a product of the planning phase; now it simply needs to be kept up to date. Second, the two diagrams are researched and built in exactly the same way. The techniques discussed in this and other chapters apply equally well to both diagrams.

However, do not be confused by talk of two diagrams. There is only *one* logical data model that consists of an E-R diagram and one data dictionary that contains information about *all* data objects. The E-R diagram can be presented using two separate views, an end-user view, called the end-user diagram, and the full E-R diagram, called a detailed diagram. The detailed diagram is just another name for the full E-R diagram.

Clouds

No matter how hard you try, certain concepts are difficult for data model readers to understand. If you are sitting next to the reader, then you can explain the difficult concepts. However, sometimes that is not possible. For example, advance copies of documents are ideally distributed before walkthroughs when no one knowledgeable is around to explain the diagram. In this situation, clouds just might be the answer.

A cloud is…well a…cloud on the E-R diagram containing text to explain difficult or complex data modeling constructs (Figure 6.8).

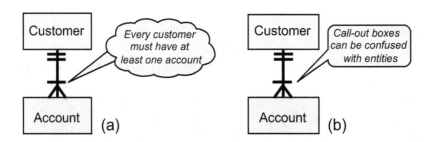

Figure 6.8 Explaining Concepts Using: (a) a Cloud
and (b) a Call-Out Box

Clouds are placed on the diagram—almost always the end-user diagram—to preempt user difficulties with the model (Figure 6.8a). Some modelers use call-out boxes or balloons—like the text boxes in comic strips—but their shape can sometimes be confused with entities (Figure 6.8b). Clouds, if done right, are never confused with legitimate data modeling graphics.

Use clouds sparingly or your logical data model will start to look like a weather map, obscuring its real purpose.

Enterprise Models

Some models are created, not just to represent an application, but an entire organization. An *enterprise model* documents the processes and/or data for an entire organization, division, or company. The *enterprise process model* is a high-level model that represents the major processes of the organization. The *enterprise data model* is a high-level E-R diagram of the information an organization uses. It is similar to the end-user diagram but with a broader scope (the entire organization) and sometimes at an even higher level of abstraction than the end-user diagram. With the exception of the level of detail, the steps to build an enterprise data model are identical to those described earlier in this book.

Using Data Modeling and CASE Tools

Systems development modeling tools are changing the way systems are built. Computer aided software engineering (CASE) tools that deal with analysis (sometimes called upper CASE) usually have a data modeling component. Sometimes this component is a powerful data-modeling tool, and other times it is little more than a means to push boxes around on a screen. Some are tied to a single data modeling technique or approach while others are more free range, allowing the data modeler to follow Chen, or IDEF1X, or any other flavors of data modeling. However, few tools are complete. Many offer a hodgepodge of techniques and diagramming conventions. The result: while they can represent one or more data modeling approaches, few tools provide discipline or alert the modeler to mistakes.

What are the advantages of using tools for data modeling? Tools allow you to:

- Make changes to an existing diagram quickly.

- Cross-reference objects, e.g., print reports showing attributes that share a domain, etc.

- View data objects from various perspectives:

    — Subject area diagrams.
    — Neighborhood diagrams.
    — Entity fragment diagrams.

- Project diagrams onto large screens for meetings.

- Move the model to other teams, phases, or tools automatically.

When can the tool be of no advantage or an outright disadvantage? When:

- Drawing the first version of a diagram—drawing the first version by hand is almost always easier.

- Preparing documentation—dictionaries existed long before CASE tools.

- It replaces thinking.

The Final Technique

Given this chapter and the previous one, it should be obvious that the most critical skill in building a logical data model is not using E-R techniques but mastering communications techniques, the third logical design principle. The best diagram in the world is useless if the information it contains never gets into the heads of its intended audience. The best data modelers always aim for clarity of message over technical prowess.

Chapter
7

Physical Database Design

Vision without action is a daydream. Action without vision is a nightmare.
~ Japanese Proverb

The most amazing achievement of the computer software industry
is its continuing cancellation of the steady and staggering gains
made by the computer hardware industry.
~ Henry Petroski (engineer, author)

Physical database design includes two separate tasks, physical data modeling and database schema definition. These tasks might be performed by one individual, call him or her the physical database designer, or by two separate individuals, the physical data modeler and the database schema designer. If you are both the logical data modeler and the physical database designer, then you know what information you require to build a database. However, in many organizations, the logical data modeler, physical data modeler, and database schema designer are three different people, possibly located in three separate and geographically dispersed organizations. In this situation, the logical data modeler has the difficult task of anticipating what the physical data modeler and the database schema designer will require.

This chapter presents a physical database design approach to understand how the information uncovered during the logical data modeling task is used to design effective databases.

The Physical Database Design Process

Physical database design consists of building a database schema from the logical data model, the logical process model, the physical data model, and the physical process model, and the systems environment (hardware, software, and network) in which the database will exist (Figure 7.1). While logical data models are very use independent, the physical database design is quite use specific. The data models provide the definition of the data and the process models document exactly how those data will be used. All four models and the systems environment are essential to good physical database design.

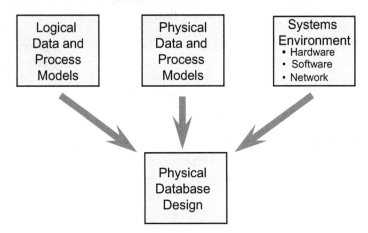

Figure 7.1 The Physical Database Design Process

The physical database design process is similar to assembling a puzzle. All the pieces are laid out at the beginning. The pieces are picked up, one at a time, examined, and their fit in the overall picture assessed. Occasionally, a piece is moved from its location as new and better-fitting pieces are studied and added to the puzzle. In similar manner, physical database design examines each process model function and maps it to the data model.

Done correctly, physical database design is an involved and iterative process that spans two phases of the system development cycle: physical design and construction (Figure 7.2).

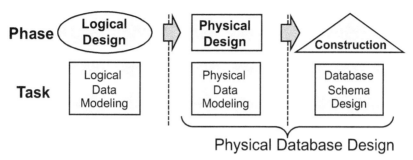

Figure 7.2 System Development Phases

Physical database design consists of four distinct steps completed across the physical design and construction system development phases.[1]

Physical data modeling is a task in the physical design development cycle. Two steps are required to transform the logical data model into a physical data model.

Step 1, *Transformation*, converts the Logical Data Model into a Basic Physical Data Model by substituting physical data modeling objects for logical data modeling ones. The output of this step is a *Basic Physical Data Model*.

Step 2, *Utilization*, uses the processes uncovered in process modeling to modify (rationalize) the Basic Physical Data Model by addressing how the data can be most efficiently used. The result is a *Rationalized Physical Data Model*

The physical data model is input for the *database schema definition* task of the construction phase of the system development cycle. Two steps are required to turn the physical data model into a working physical database design.

Step 3, *Formalization*, takes the Rationalized Physical Data Model and applies to it the rules and features of the file manager or database management system that will be used, creating a *Functional Database Design*.

Step 4, *Customization*, works on improving the performance of the database using all of the file manager or database management system features and tools available. The result is an *Enhanced Database Design*.

The complete physical database design process is rather complex, spanning two systems development phases, consisting of four distinct steps, each with their own set of deliverables (Figure 7.3).

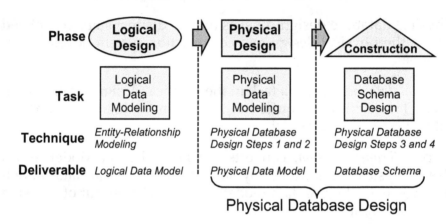

Phase	Logical Design	Physical Design	Construction
Task	Logical Data Modeling	Physical Data Modeling	Database Schema Design
Technique	*Entity-Relationship Modeling*	*Physical Database Design Steps 1 and 2*	*Physical Database Design Steps 3 and 4*
Deliverable	*Logical Data Model*	*Physical Data Model*	*Database Schema*

Physical Database Design

Figure 7.3 Physical Database Design Spans the Physical Design and Construction System Development Phases

The remainder of this chapter lays out exactly what happens in the Physical Data Modeling and Database Schema Definition tasks.

Physical Design: Physical Data Modeling

The best way to understand the physical database design process is by example. Figure 7.4 is a logical data model for a Stock Brokerage Securities Processing System.

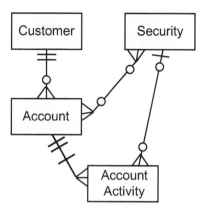

Figure 7.4 Securities Processing Logical Data Model

Customers can open Accounts and trade Securities (stock), with each transaction recorded in the Account Activity entity.

Step 1 Transformation—Convert the Logical Data Model to a Basic Physical Data Model

This is the easiest step. To transform a logical data model to a basic physical data model, entities become record types, attributes become fields, and relationships become database links (Table 7.1). Because the database management system has not yet been specified—that occurs in Step 3—non-database management specific terms are used. Words such as tables, sets, and segments (all tied to specific database management systems) are avoided.

Table 7.1 Converting Logical Data Modeling Objects
to Physical Data Modeling Objects

LOGICAL DATA OBJECT —> PHYSICAL DATA OBJECT		
Entity	—>	Record Type
Relationship	—>	Link
Attribute	—>	Field (Data Element)
Cardinality	—>	Cardinality
Modality	—>	Modality

The conventions for logical data modeling objects, such as naming rules, continue in Step 1. For example, record type names start with a capital letter, and field names are in all capitals, spaces allowed, etc.

Most diagram graphics are the same (Figure 7.5)—a box for a record type and a line for a link between record types. Cardinality and modality are the same; however, the trident is now an arrow with the arrowhead pointing at the many end of the link.

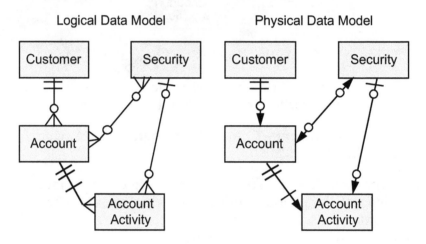

Figure 7.5 Logical and Physical Data Models

Many-to-many and n-ary links (relationships) remain unchanged.

The output of Step 1 is a *basic physical data model,* although the modeler might hear other terms such as a *data structure diagram* or *Bachman diagram*[2].

Step 2 Utilization—Apply the Processes Documented in the Process Model to the Basic Physical Data Model

Below is the Stock Brokerage Securities Processing System process, Fetch Security Activity.

Process 1: Fetch Security Activity
For each Security occurrence, give its activity (Account Activity), including information on the securities (Security) and account holder (Account)

For physical database design purposes, the process Fetch Security Activity can be rewritten in a more database-specific style called a *usage scenario*.

Usage Scenario 1: Fetch Security Activity
1.1 Enter database at Security
1.2 Read Account Activity for each Security
1.3 Read Account for each Account Activity

Each line of the usage scenario starts with a command.

- **Enter** (E)—initial transaction entry into the database (initial database call).
- **Read** (R)—fetching a record from inside the database (navigation).
- **Insert** (I)—adding a record.
- **Update** (U)—modifying a record.
- **Delete** (D)—erasing a record.

The usage scenario can then be *mapped* onto the physical data model, creating a *usage map* (Figure 7.6).

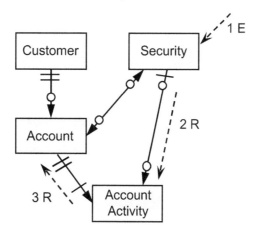

Figure 7.6 Usage Map for Fetch Security Activity

The dashed arrows in Figure 7.6 indicate where the database is entered and the navigation within the database from there. The numbers indicate the sequence of that navigation. The diagram shows that the database is entered at a Security record occurrence, then the corresponding Account Activity record occurrences are read, and then the corresponding Account occurrences are read.

The output for this transaction might look something like Figure 7.7.

SECURITY	ACTIVITY	ACCOUNT
Siddall Ltd	Buy 100 Shares	12345
	Sell 200 Shares	45458
Rowley Inc	Buy 200 Shares	25466
	Buy 100 Shares	24543
Chatterton Inc	Buy 140 Shares	43435
	Sell 300 Shares	90567
		45321

Figure 7.7 Report Output for Fetch Security Activity

Process models can involve pages of information detailing calculations and directions for displaying information with few or no references to database activity. Usage scenarios allow the physical database designer to cut through the non-database relevant process model minutia and exclusively focus on database calls, often reducing pages of process model information to a half-page of database commands.

The value of the usage scenario becomes evident when a second process is added to the system. For example, take process two, Fetch Customer Activity.

Process 2: Fetch Customer Activity
For each Customer occurrence, fetch all Account occurrences and within each Account occurrence, fetch all Account Activity

The usage scenario for Fetch Customer Activity might look like the following:

Usage Scenario 2: Fetch Customer Activity
2.1 Enter database at Customer
2.2 Read Account occurrence for each Customer
2.3 Read Account Activity for each Account

Figure 7.8 is the usage map (also called a *usage scenario diagram*) for Process 2, Fetch Customer Activity.

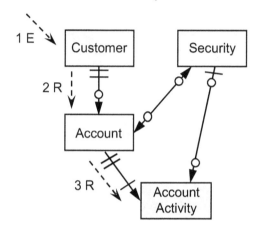

Figure 7.8 Usage Map for Fetch Customer Activity

The output for Process 2, Fetch Customer Activity, might look something like Figure 7.9.

CUSTOMER	ACCOUNT	ACTIVITY	SECURITY
Cassidy	43456	Buy 100 Shares	Siddall Ltd
		Sell 200 Shares	Rowley Inc
Longabaugh	34667	Buy 200 Shares	Chatterton
		Buy 100 Shares	Ronco Ltd.
Place	18896	Buy 140 Shares	Rowley Inc
		Sell 300 Shares	Siddall Ltd
			Ronco Ltd.

Figure 7.9 Report Output for Fetch Customer Activity

Two or more usage scenarios can be combined into the single *combined usage map* in Figure 7.10.

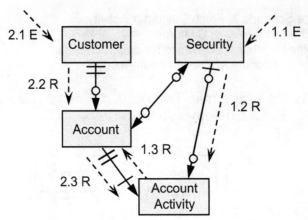

Figure 7.10 Combined Usage Map

There should be one usage map for each usage scenario. Mapping all of the usage maps onto a single page creates a *combined usage map*. A 50-record-type database with 50 usage scenarios can result in a rather complicated but very important combined usage map. However, even with only two usage scenarios important information becomes clear. Looking at Figure 7.10 it is obvious that the link between Security and Account is unnecessary and can be eliminated.

The output of Step 2 is a modified or *rationalized physical data model* reflecting how the data are used (Figure 7.11).

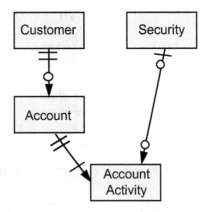

Figure 7.11 Rationalized Physical Data Model

The rationalized physical data model is THE physical data model produced as the deliverable of the physical design phase of the system development cycle. This is the easy part. In the construction phase of the system development cycle, the physical data model becomes a real physical database design.

This completes the physical design section of physical database design. The next two steps, where the physical data model becomes a database schema, are part of the construction development phase.

Construction: Database Schema Definition

Step 3 Formalization—Modify the Rationalized Physical Data Model to Comply With the Rules of the Selected File or Database Management System

Between Step 2 and Step 3, the organization must choose or confirm the information management system that will be used, be it a simple file manager or a complete database management system. Step 3, Formalization, involves making the rationalized physical data model design conform to the rules and features of the chosen information manager. For example, if the information manager does not support many-to-many links, then the designer must insert junction records to make each many-to-many link into two one-to-many links.

The simple Stock Brokerage Securities Processing System, consisting of only four record types and three links makes this a very simple task; however, the procedure is the same, regardless of size or complexity.

Assume that the organization's information manager is the *Imaginary Database Management System,* and it has the following properties and features (Table 7.2).

Table 7.2 Imaginary Database Management System
Rules and Features

RULE	ACTION REQUIRED
Many-to-many links not allowed	Insert junction record
Every record must have a primary key	Promote identifier to primary key Create primary key where there is no identifier
Use NOT NULL to enforce modality	Create foreign keys
Spaces not allowed in names	Substitute an underscore for spaces

To make the rationalized physical data model a *Functional Database Design* for the Imaginary Database Management System, the physical database designer must:

- Make the data element CUSTOMER_NUMBER in the Customer record type the primary key of Customer.

- Make the data element SECURITY_ID in the Security record type the primary key of Security.

- Make the data element ACCOUNT_NUMBER in the Account record type the primary key of Account.

- Create a primary key for Account_Activity by concatenating the field ACCOUNT_NUMBER from Account with the created field DATE_TIME from the system timestamp.

- To accommodate the mandatory relationship between Customer and Account, create a duplicate field in Account named CUSTOMER_NUMBER and specify that the field CUSTOMER_NUMBER in Account cannot be null.

- To accommodate the mandatory relationship between Account and Account_Activity, duplicate the field ACCOUNT_NUMBER in Account Activity and state that it cannot be null.

The result of Step 3 is a *Functional Database Design* (Figure 7.12).

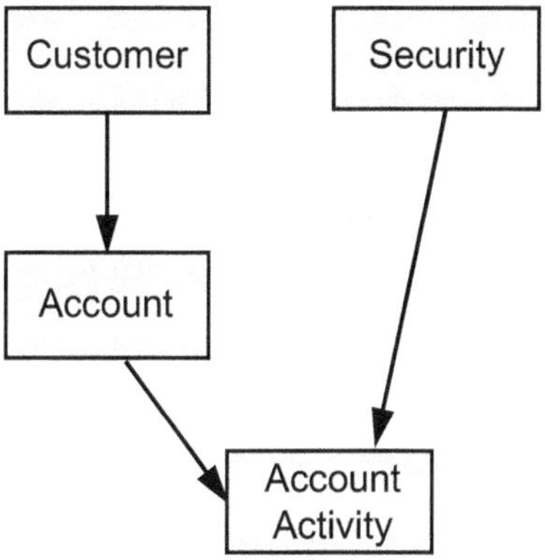

Figure 7.12 Functional Database Design

Note that the Functional Database Design created for the Imaginary Database Management System does not support certain logical data modeling features such as:

- Many-to-many and unary relationships. They must be converted to one-to-many links.

- Associative entities (which are attributed relationships). They become standard record types.

- Spaces in names are not allowed, so Account Activity becomes Account_Activity and ACCOUNT NUMBER becomes ACCOUNT_NUMBER.

The systems designers either must forgo these features or implement them some other way, such as using database procedures, triggers, or application code.

Lastly, the designer must create a database schema using the *data description language* for the organization's database management system. Table 7.3 contains a few lines of the code necessary to create the Stock Brokerage Securities Processing System database using the Imaginary Database Management System.

Table 7.3 Code Fragment to Create Database Schema

```
•
•
CREATE TABLE CUSTOMER (
        CUSTOMER_NAME CHAR(30) NOT NULL,
        CUSTOMER_NUMBER CHAR(8) NOT NULL PRIMARY KEY
            UNIQUE,
        CUSTOMER_STREET_NUMBER CHAR(6),
        CUSTOMER_STREET_NAME CHAR(24),
        CUSTOMER_CITY CHAR(24),
        CUSTOMER_STATE_PROVINCE CHAR(2),
•
•
```

Step 3 deliverables include the *functional database design* or *functional database schema* (database definition).

Step 4 Customization—Improve the Performance of the Functional Database Design

If the first three steps were properly completed, then the organization should have a working database. However, a blessing, as well as a curse, of most database management systems is their ability to function even when poorly designed. The drawback of a poor design is poor performance. Luckily, most database management systems have features and tools to improve performance. Step 4, Customization, improves the performance of the database schema created in Step 3.

If there is one word to describe physical database design, it is TRADEOFF. The physical database designer must understand each process requesting database services, calculate the resources required to satisfy that request, adjudicate competing requests for services from multiple processes, and create a physical database design that provides the best all-around solution. In the world of database management systems, the most expensive resource is a physical I/O—the reading, modifying, or deleting a physical record on disk. Although the numbers vary based on the speed of the computer and the disk, a safe assumption that we will use is that reading a record from disk (physical I/O) is about 1,000 times slower than reading a record from main memory (logical I/O). For the simple example presented in this chapter, the assumption is that reducing physical I/Os is the only option for improving database efficiency. In the real world, there are other factors that should be considered for improving database efficiency (such as the number of servers, the network speed, the CPU speed, etc.); however, even in the real world, physical I/O is, in almost every case, the number one resource consumer.

The designer needs to know what tools exist in the toolshed—the features of the database management system. The Imaginary Database Management System has two features of importance: hashing and clustering.

- Hashing is a technique for storing a record occurrence on a database page based on the value of its key. (If the page where a record is stored is known, then the system can directly access the record, avoiding the need to read costly indices.) For example, assume the key of the Customer occurrence is "12345678," and there are 900 pages (storage areas) in the database. The simplest hashing scheme is to divide the key of the desired occurrence by the number of pages (in this case, 12345678/900 = 13,717 with a remainder of 378). Add 1 to the remainder (379), and this is the page the database management system should use to store the occurrence.

- Clustering is a technique for storing a record occurrence on the same database page as another record occurrence—often the record that is accessed just prior to the target record. For example, to reduce physical I/O, store the Account Activity occurrences on the same database page as their related Account occurrence. Then, assuming there is sufficient space on the page, Account and Account_Activity can be fetched with a single physical I/O.

Data volumes (the number of occurrences of each record type) are important for physical database design. This information should be easily obtainable from the data dictionary if the data and process modelers did their job. Table 7.4 contains the actual or anticipated volume information for the Stockbroker system.

Table 7.4 Record Type Volumes

RECORD TYPE	OCCURRENCES
Customer	30,000
Account	50,000
Account Activity	500,000
Security	3,000

Physical Database Design for Process 1: Fetch Security Activity

Step 4 design starts with the first process, its usage scenario, and the process transaction volumes (Table 7.5) from the logical process model.

Table 7.5 Process 1 Transaction Volumes

Process 1: Fetch Security Activity

Volume: 3,000 transactions per day
Batch 3,000
Priority: Low

Go back to the first database process, Fetch Security Activity, and its usage scenario (Figure 7.6). The most efficient way (minimum physical I/O) to execute the process is to enter the database at Security, navigate to the relevant Account_Activity record occurrences, and then to the Account that holds those securities.

A simple way to design the database is to store each record type using a hash key. By hashing on the record type key, the record occurrence can ideally be fetched with a single physical I/O. Actually, the number of I/Os is slightly higher. If the record occurrence is on the correct page, then one physical I/O is required. However, if there is no room on the page, then the database management system must go to an overflow page. If page overflow occurs 10 percent of the time then, on average, a fetch will require 1.1 reads, so fetching each Security occurrence will require 1.1 physical I/Os. For each Security occurrence there are, on average, 167 Account_Activity occurrences (500,000 divided by 3,000) that require 184 (167 x 1.1) additional physical I/Os per Security occurrence. The 167 Account_Activity occurrences require an additional 184 physical I/Os to fetch the corresponding Account record. Multiply the sum by the number of Security occurrences, and you have 1,107,000 physical I/Os to complete the process. However, there is a cheaper way to execute Process 1 that requires considerably less physical I/O.

For this second approach, the Security record type is hashed, so fetching a Security record occurrence takes, on average, 1.1 physical I/Os. That has not changed. The Account_Activity occurrences can be stored on the same physical database page (clustered) as their corresponding Security occurrence. If every Account_Activity record is stored on the same page as its corresponding Security record, then no additional physical I/Os are required. However, if there is not sufficient room, then additional I/Os will be needed. There are, on average, 167 Account_Activity occurrences for each Security occurrence, with a 90-percent chance that the Account_Activity record will be on the same page; therefore, to fetch all 167 records requires 16.7 physical I/Os.

Ideally, it is most efficient to store an Account record on the same database page as its corresponding Account_Activity records. However, the Imaginary Database Management System does not allow a record occurrence to be clustered around another clustered record occurrence or a record occurrence to which it is not directly linked. Therefore, fetching the Account record occurrence corresponding to each Account_Activity record requires using an Account hash key. Navigating from the 167 Account_Activity records for each Security record to its corresponding Account record requires, on average, 183.7 physical I/Os.

The total number of physical I/Os required per Security occurrence (called a *physical I/O path*) is 201.5. To produce the Fetch Security activity report for all securities is 604,400 physical I/Os.

The cluster feature allows the design of a database that is almost twice as efficient (604,400 versus 1,107,000 physical I/Os) as one without.

A very important component of a physical database design is the *Database Design Rationale,* a sort of physical database designer journal or diary that documents the reason for every physical database design decision. The design rationale is not only useful for documenting and reviewing a physical database design but helps the physical database designer better understand how current or future changes will affect database performance.

The Database Design Rationale for Process 1 looks something like the following.

Account_Activity Clustered Around Security
Process 1: Fetch Security Activity

Record Type: Security, Entry point for process
Includes Field: SECURITY_ID *<Only list fields relevant to the process>*
Storage Method: Hashed, Hashed Field: SECURITY_ID
Access: Hash Key
Navigation: To Account_Activity (By scanning Security database page for records with corresponding SECURITY_IDs) *<Where to go after fetching Security occurrence>*

Record Type: Account_Activity
Includes Field: SECURITY_ID
Includes Field: ACCOUNT_NUMBER
Storage Method: Cluster, Cluster Key: SECURITY_ID
Access: Scan Page where Security is stored. *<Fetch Account_Activity records by scanning the Security database page>*
Navigation: To Account (Using ACCOUNT_NUMBER as hashed field of Account)

Record Type: Account
Includes Field: ACCOUNT_NUMBER
Storage Method: Hashed, Hashed Field: ACCOUNT_NUMBER
Access: Hash Key

Table 7.6 shows the output of the Process 1 analysis.

Table 7.6 Physical I/O Requirements for
Process 1: Fetch Security Activity

RECORD TYPE	NUMBER	PATH NUMBER	HASH I/O	INDEX I/O	TOTAL PATH	TOTAL I/O*
Security	3,000	1	1.1	0	1.1	3,300
Account_Activity	500,000	167	0.1	0	16.7	50,000
Account	50,000	167	1.1	0	183.7	551,100
TOTAL						604,400

*Note, The results for TOTAL PATH times 3,000 Security occurrences.

Note that the Database Design Rationale includes comments (set off in <>) regarding the reasons for certain decisions. This not only helps others understand why certain things are done, but also helps future designers who might have to modify the physical database design to accommodate new requirements.

The physical database design for Process 1 looks like the one in Figure 7.13. However, hold off calling it the *Enhanced Database Design* (the output of Step 4, Customization) until all the processes (and usage scenarios) are analyzed.

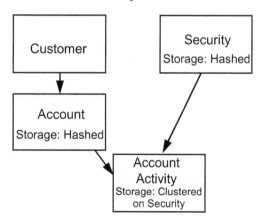

Figure 7.13 Physical Database Design for
Process 1: Fetch Security Activity

There is a second process the physical database design must support, Process 2: Fetch Customer Activity.

Physical Database Design for Process 2: Fetch Customer Activity

The second Stockbroker process, Process 2: Fetch Customer Activity, can now be added to the physical database design. Table 7.7 gives the process transaction volumes from the logical process model.

Table 7.7 Process 2 Transaction Volumes

Process 2: Fetch Customer Activity

> Volume: 30,000 transactions per day
> Batch 30,000
> Priority: Low

Process 2 presents some new challenges. The Imaginary Database Management System does not allow a record to be clustered around another record if is not directly linked to it. Process 2's usage scenario says that the database is entered at Customer and then navigates to Account and finally Account_Activity, so the design question becomes: is Account clustered around Customer or is Account_Activity clustered around Account? Given the constraints of the database management system, both are not possible.

Luckily, a little simple arithmetic can answer the question.

Just part of Process 2 Database Design Rationale is below.

> Process 2: Fetch Customer Activity
> •
> •
> Record Type: Account
> Includes Field: ACCOUNT_NUMBER
> Includes Field: CUSTOMER_NUMBER (potential)
> Storage Method: Hashed, Hashed Field: ACCOUNT_NUMBER

<Process 1 had Account stored using ACCOUNT_NUMBER as a hashed field. Issue: How do you navigate to Account from Customer? Must have either Account clustered on Customer, negating Process 1, or a second option that allows Account to remain hashed. If the database management system allows pointers (example a CODASYL system), then a set can be established allowing pointers from Customer to Account. If the database management system does not allow pointers (example a relational system), then CUSTOMER_NUMBER must be duplicated in Account and an index must be created in Account using CUSTOMER_NUMBER as the index key>
Access: Index
Index Key: CUSTOMER_NUMBER
Navigation: To Account_Activity
-
-

Table 7.8 shows the output of the Process 2 analysis.

Table 7.8 Physical I/O Requirements for Process 2: Fetch Customer Activity

RECORD TYPE	NUMBER	PATH NUMBER	HASH I/O	INDEX I/O*	TOTAL PATH	TOTAL I/O
Customer	30,000	1	1.1	0	1.1	33,000
Account	50,000	1.7	0	3	5.0	150,000
Account_Activity	500,000	16.7	0	4	66.7	2,000,000
TOTAL						2,183,000

*Note, this example does not calculate index physical I/O. However, that is a calculation physical database designers must perform.

Two indices must be added to the physical database design. Indices are graphically indicated by the use of a triangle, labeled with the index key, attached to the record type (Figure 7.14).

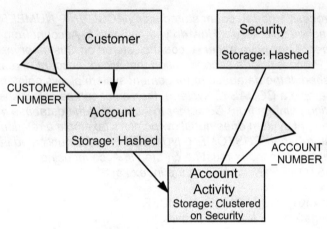

Figure 7.14 Physical Database Design for Processes 1 and 2

Combining the totals for processes 1 and 2 results in 2,787,400 physical I/Os. Call this *Option 1: Cluster Account_Activity Around Security* because there is a second option, *Option 2: Cluster Account_Activity Around Account.*

Option 2: Cluster Account_Activity Around Account

Option 1 clustered Account_Activity around Security. Option 2 removes that clustering and instead clusters Account_Activity around Account (Figure 7.15).

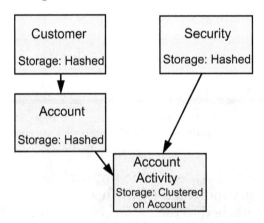

Figure 7.15 Physical Database Design for Option 2: Account_Activity Clustered Around Account

Parts of the Database Design Rationale for Option 2 are below.

> Option 2: Account_Activity Clustered Around Account
> *Process 1: Fetch Security Activity*
> •
> •
> Record Type Account_Activity
> Includes Field: SECURITY_ID
> Includes Field: ACCOUNT_NUMBER
> Storage Method: Cluster, Cluster Key: ACCOUNT_NUMBER
> *<Problem: Because record is clustered on Account, Security needs an alternative way to get to Account_Activity. Answer: Pointers or an Index on SECURITY_ID in Account_Activity.>*
> Access: Index
> Index Key: SECURITY_ID
> Navigation: To Account
> •
> •
> Record Type: Account
> Includes Field: ACCOUNT_NUMBER
> Storage Method: Hashed, Hashed Field: ACCOUNT_NUMBER
> Access: Scan Page where Account_Activity is stored. *<Because Account_Activity records are stored clustered using ACCOUNT_NUMBER as the clustering key, a simple scan of the database page for Account_Activity will find corresponding Account records. >*
> •
> •

Table 7.9 shows the output of the Option 2 Process 1 analysis.

Table 7.9 Physical I/O Requirements for Option 2,
Process 1: Fetch Security Activity

RECORD TYPE	NUMBER	PATH NUMBER	HASH I/O	INDEX I/O	TOTAL PATH	TOTAL I/O
Security	3,000	1	1.1	0	1.1	3,300
Account_Activity	500,000	167	0	4	666.7	2,000,000
Account	50,000	167	0.1	0	16.7	50,100
TOTAL						2,053,400

Applying the analysis to Option 2 Process 2 leads to this fragment of the Database Design Rationale.

> Option 2: Account_Activity Clustered Around Account
> Process 2: Fetch Customer Activity
> •
> •
> Record Type: Account
> Includes Field: ACCOUNT_NUMBER
> Includes Field: CUSTOMER_NUMBER
> Storage Method: Hashed, Hashed Field: ACCOUNT_NUMBER
> *< Because Imaginary Database Management System does not allow clustered records to have other records clustered to them, then either Account can be stored clustered to Customer or Account_Activity can be clustered around Account, but not both. Because the ratio of Account to Account_Activity is higher than the ratio of Customer to Account, the former is chosen as the clustering scheme.>*
> Access: Index, Index Key: CUSTOMER_NUMBER
> Navigation: To Account_Activity (Scan of Account database page for Account_Activity records with corresponding ACCOUNT_NUMBER)
> •
> •

Table 7.10 shows the output of the Option 2 Process 2 analysis.

Table 7.10 Physical I/O Requirements for
Option 2, Process 2: Fetch Customer Activity

RECORD TYPE	NUMBER	PATH NUMBER	HASH I/O	INDEX I/O	TOTAL PATH	TOTAL I/O
Customer	30,000	1	1.1	0	1.1	33,000
Account	50,000	1.7	0	3	5.0	150,000
Account_Activity	500,000	16.7	0.1	0	1.7	50,000
TOTAL						233,000

The choice between Option 1 and Option 2 is a simple arithmetic problem as shown in Table 7.11.

Table 7.11 Comparison of Options 1 and 2

Processes	Option 1: Cluster Account_Activity Around Security (Physical I/O)	Option 2: Cluster Account_Activity Around Account (Physical I/O)
Process 1: Fetch Security Activity	604,400	2,053,400
Process 2: Fetch Customer Activity	2,183,000	233,000
TOTAL	2,787,400	2,286,400

Option 2 requires a half-million fewer I/Os than Option 1—a 22 percent improvement. Based on these numbers, the most efficient physical database design, based on Option 2, is shown in Figure 7.16.

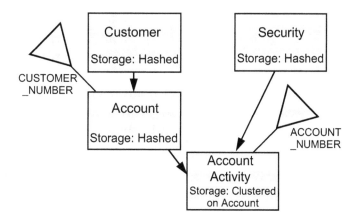

Figure 7.16 Enhanced Database Design

This is where physical database designers earn their wings. As mentioned earlier, the one word that best describes physical database design is TRADEOFF. The physical database designer must decide to tune the database to favor either Option 1 or Option 2.

The stockbroker example is embarrassingly simple. It involves a database with four record types and two processes, and both processes are batch processes with identical priorities. Add in the feature-poor Imaginary Database Management System, and the result is a simple classroom exercise. In the real world, the physical database designer might face 50 record types, 20 processes, some online and some batch, with different priorities, supporting different demanding users, and a database management system with a dozen or more storage and access features. The physical database designer must juggle all of these to come up with the best compromise for competing requests for service.

Tradeoffs are the toughest part of physical database design and the part that requires the most input from the logical data and process models. The challenge facing both logical and physical staff is identifying exactly what information the designer requires to perform these critical tradeoffs.

How Logical Data Modeling and Physical Database Design Differ

As noted earlier, logical data modeling is quite different from physical database design. Whereas logical design is concerned with abstracting and constructing a representation of an organization, physical design is concerned with transforming the various analysis models into a physical reality. The logical data modeler must be adept at interviewing staff, drawing out important information, and conceptualizing the meaning of the raw data. The physical designer, on the other hand, must be able to:

• Merge a number of models dealing with data, processes, and the systems environment (hardware, software, and network).

• Resolve conflicts for resources from competing applications and/or users.

• Produce a workable physical design of the system that maximizes benefits at minimum cost (Table 7.12).

Table 7.12 Differences Between Logical Data Modeling
and Physical Database Design Skills

NECESSARY LOGICAL DATA MODELING SKILLS	NECESSARY PHYSICAL DATABASE DESIGN SKILLS
• Conceptualization (see world logically)	• Understanding of hardware, software, and network usage
• Abstraction	• Concrete thinking
• Interview skills	• Ability to work well with systems staff
• Good "people" skills	• Ability to uncover and manage tradeoffs (balance competing needs)
• Ability to uncover facts	

The most important skill the designer must exhibit is the ability to balance competing needs and correctly manage the tradeoffs.

The Role of the Logical Data Modeler in Physical Database Design

The information necessary to make the all-important judgment calls is not always available to the physical database designer. Sketchy methodologies, missing or incomplete analysis, and simple technical or clerical errors can conceal important information, leaving the physical database designer in the dark when making critical decisions. The logical data modeler should be aware of these challenges and work to keep the physical designer informed.

Information that the logical data modeler should give to the physical database designer is of three types:

• *Formal deliverables defined by the systems development methodology, techniques, and tools.* These deliverables are required outputs of the project and are usually determined by the organization, methodology vendor, or project team before the project starts. Simply stated, they are what you have to formally do to say you are formally done.

- *Informal outputs, such as information that might be required by the physical designer but is not included in the methodology, technique, or tool deliverables.* This includes logical data modeling reports, worksheets, and notes created during logical data modeling that are not part of the formal deliverables handed off for physical database design.

- *Informal notes, suggestions, or tips* the logical designer feels are, or might be, important for the physical designer. This category includes insights that the logical modeler wants to share with the physical designers. The subject can be logical or physical in nature. In fact, the subject can be anything that may support the physical designer in fulfilling the physical database design task.

In the case of informal outputs and notes, the logical designer has the opportunity to communicate any information that does not fit into formal deliverables, i.e., information that is needed but cannot, or should not, be bundled into a predetermined (formal) package. An example is non-unique attributes that are almost unique (candidates for use as a primary key or secondary index) or unique attributes that seem stable but change values frequently (not a good candidate for a key). This information, which might be missing or buried in the formal deliverables, can be invaluable to the physical database designer.

As has been stressed time and again in this book, the logical data modeler should not be involved in physical design issues. However, being human, thoughts and, sometimes, clever ideas pop into a data modeler's head uninvited. If those thoughts are about physical design, and might be useful to the physical designer, then, rather than discarding them, communicate them. When a flash of brilliance appears about how something should be done physically, the modeler should do three things:

- Write it down.

- Ignore it when building the logical data model.

- And, at the end of logical data modeling, review the bits collected and pass on to the physical designer the ones that still make sense as comments or informal suggestions.

The tasks performed by the logical data modeler, physical data modeler, and database schema designer differ. The deliverables they produce are different. Their backgrounds and training are often different. However, they all have the same goal: to produce a database that meets the user's functional requirements in an effective and efficient way. Learning just a bit about what the other guy does can only add to the success of the team's efforts.

CHAPTER NOTES

[1]The physical database design approach is taken from:
George Tillmann, *Usage-Driven Database Design: From Logical Data Modeling through Physical Schema Definition*, Apress, 2017.

[2]Charles Bachman, "Data Structure Diagrams," *DataBase: A Quarterly Newsletter of SIGBDP*, Vol. 1, No. 2, Summer 1969, pp. 4–10.

Chapter
8

What About…?

No one is dumb who is curious.
The people who don't ask questions remain clueless throughout their lives.
~ Neil deGrasse Tyson

There are known unknowns.
That is to say, we know there are some things we do not know.
But there are unknown unknowns, the ones we don't know we don't know.
~ Donald Rumsfeld (former US Secretary of Defense)

If you have read the book to this point, you probably feel that you have a good grasp of the Entity-Relationship Model. However, if you are like most new modelers, you still have some questions. This chapter contains the questions most frequently asked by new modelers and my answers. The chapter is divided into sections on derived data, identifiers and keys, normalization, other data models, resolving many-to-many relationships, and data warehouses and big data.

WHAT ABOUT…DERIVED DATA?

You model a business using logical modeling. You model a computer system using physical modeling. You model the data in a business using logical data modeling, and you model the processes in a business using logical process modeling. All simple and straightforward—except when it's not.

The problem? Explain cardinality to an end-user or business analyst, and you rarely have a problem. Explain to them that derived data is not shown on the E-R diagram and you might start a range war. For whatever reason, some end users and technical staff have an emotional attachment to derived data that they don't have to other logical design concepts. The sole remedy is to explain in detail why derived data are treated the way they are. This section should help.

Derived Data: Derived Attributes

There are processes that look like data, act like data, and confuse some very smart people. These processes are called derived data. Remember from Chapter 2, a data attribute can be primitive or derived. A primitive attribute is one that expresses an atomic or non-decomposable fact (value) about the entity, as in the COLOR is "blue." A derived attribute is calculated from one or more primitive attributes (atomic facts), or other derived attributes, by the application of an algorithm. For example, in an accounts receivable system, INVOICE AMOUNT is derived because it can be calculated by adding up the ITEM AMOUNT values.

The three traditional arguments against modeling derived data are that it:

- Is redundant.
- Takes up database storage space.
- Limits the choices of physical designers.

Many modelers say that TOTAL AMOUNT ORDERED is redundant because it can be calculated from the individual line items. This redundancy is undesirable because it can lead to inconsistencies if the value of TOTAL AMOUNT ORDERED does not equal the sum of LINE ITEM AMOUNT. Put simply, the argument is that if data are stored only once, then there are no inconsistencies.

The second argument is that because it is redundant, derived data unnecessarily take up storage space (i.e., on disk or tape) and increases storage costs.

The third argument goes as follows: The decision about whether a data object should be stored or calculated is a physical design issue. The relevant questions deal with the cost/benefit tradeoffs between the storage space required to house the redundant data and the I/O and CPU cycles necessary to calculate them every time they are needed. It is argued that if the derived data are left off the data model, the physical designer can always turn it into stored data if he or she deems it desirable. However, if derived data are part of the data model, then the physical designer might not know they are derived and therefore, not know there is an option either to store or calculate the data. Thus, placing derived data on the data model limits the options open to the designer.

These arguments are true but not very compelling. The redundancy argument ignores the fact that redundant data items can only be inconsistent when some or all of them are wrong; however, if they are wrong, they are wrong whether they are in the model once or multiple times. Redundancy, in fact, points out incorrect data that might otherwise go undetected.

It is true that storing derived data in the database increases storage costs. However, the argument is misplaced. Issues such as database storage should not be part of logical design and should be left to physical design (Separation—the first logical design principle).

The third argument is correct, but it assumes that there are no other ways to communicate the derived nature of the data object to the physical designers. However, there are numerous alternative methods of saying that data are derived without dropping them from the data model (Communication—the third logical design principle).

The notion that those who argue against derived data also believe they should not exist is a common misconception. Derived data opponents are merely against placing them in an entity and on the E-R diagram. They say that derived data are really the restatement of data that already exist in the model in one or more entities. To include them on the E-R diagram corrupts the fundamental or atomic nature of the diagram. However, information about derived data, if that information is a legitimate end-user concept, should be the data dictionary.

Stated simply—the reason not to place derived data on the E-R diagram is that derived data are not data at all; rather, they are part of a process, and as a process, they should be handled by logical process modeling (Distinction—the second logical design principle).

Derived Data as Process

Derived data do not behave like data. For example, you can completely understand primitive data with a definition; however, to understand derived data requires a formula or algorithm. Look at the example:

> PAYMENT REQUIRED for ACCOUNT NUMBER = '1234' is the sum of the values of LINE ITEM AMOUNT for that account times the CUSTOMER DISCOUNT which is calculated from ORDERS THIS PERIOD.

To understand PAYMENT REQUIRED requires a formula, action diagram, or pseudo code. However, formulas, action diagrams, and pseudo code are properties of processes, not data. Therefore, the real problem with putting derived data on the E-R diagram is that they are not data at all. They are, instead, the result of a process that applies a set of rules to data values, from fundamental attributes that might exist in multiple different entity types, to calculate the derived data values (Figure 8.1).

Where Would You Put Derived Attributes?

Another reason not to put derived data on the E-R diagram is, where do you put it? For example, assume that the derived attribute TOTAL AMOUNT DUE is calculated from the primitive attribute ORDER AMOUNT, which is a property of the Invoice entity, and the primitive attribute DISCOUNT EARNED, which is a property of the Customer entity. Which entity is the derived attribute TOTAL AMOUNT DUE a property of and located in? Invoice? Customer? Some new entity created just to store the derived attribute? The correct answer is, none of the above.

Derived Data and Database Design

Whether derived attributes are stored in the database or calculated every time they are required is a mathematical question. The physical database designer calculates the resource costs to store the derived data, compares them with the resource costs to calculate them every time they are required, and chooses the less expensive option. The only real question is how does the physical database designer know the data are derived?

Primitive Data Can Be Understood
by Their Definition

Attribute Definition

    Attribute Name: ACCOUNT NUMBER

    Definition: An identifier of an approved account of any status. The Accounts Payable Dept. assigns account numbers.

However, Derived Data Require
a Formula or Algorithm

Calculate Total Amount Ordered

    Get Accounts Payable Entity

        For each ACCOUNT NUMBER

            Sum LINE ITEM AMOUNT giving
            TOTAL AMOUNT ORDERED

        End

    End

End

Figure 8.1 Derived Data Require a Process

If derived data are not on the E-R diagram, then how are they represented in the database design process? This can be a problem. Many data modelers make the mistake of so efficiently excluding derived data from development documentation that physical designers do not even know these data exist.

The solution to this problem is relatively simple. Derived data should not be on the E-R diagram (not be assigned to an entity or relationship); nevertheless, they should be defined in the data dictionary. The dictionary should explicitly state that the attribute is derived and give the name of the process (action diagram, data-flow diagram, etc.) that defines it.

Integrated tools allow for process information, such as action diagrams or data-flow diagrams, to be associated with derived data. Tools that only support data modeling might not allow for such documentation. The result can be a bit messy but not impossible. For example, if the tool requires all attributes to be associated with an entity, the data modeler might create one or more dummy entities to house derived attributes (Figure 8.2). Think of it as artistic license.

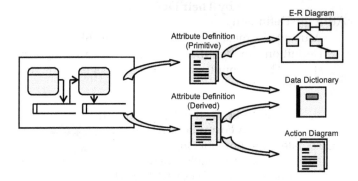

Figure 8.2 Location of Derived Data

If derived data are properly documented, then the physical database designers know that derived data exist, where they are used, and how they are calculated. They are then in a position to intelligently introduce derived data into the database design process.

Derived Data: Derived Entities

Not all derived data are attributes; they can be entities as well. Take the example of a securities firm where the business users want the entity Portfolio included on the E-R diagram. The problem is that a portfolio is simply a view of the assets held by an account. The data modeler must understand both the business definition of a portfolio and the logical data modeling definition of derived data. In this case, a portfolio includes all the occurrences of the Stock entity that are related to a specific Account instance. No additional entity is called for.

Derived attributes can cause derived entities. In the TOTAL AMOUNT DUE example, some modelers or users might call for the creation of a new entity just to store the derived attribute.

The data modeler has broader latitude with the end-user diagram than with the detailed diagram. If the derived data are very important to the user and if the user is persistent in that data being included in the model, the data modeler can always include them on the end-user diagram.

Who should place derived data in the data dictionary? This answer is: it depends. The responsibility for entering derived data into the dictionary should be the first person to come across them. If the logical data modeler is the first one to come across the derived data, then it is his or her responsibility to record that data in the data dictionary. Regardless of who finds the derived data first, their existence should be communicated to all modelers, logical and physical. Derived data must be handled as a process to satisfy the second logical design principle (Distinction) and their existence made known to all logical modelers to satisfy the third logical design principle (Communication).

WHAT ABOUT...IDENTIFIERS AND KEYS?

A sharp eye should notice that keys are not mentioned in any discussion of logical data modeling. That is for a very good and important reason. Keys are not, and nor should they be, any part of logical data modeling. Keys are part of physical database design. If, and when, the logical data model is to be transformed into a physical database design, then the discussion of keys is appropriate. The function of logical data modeling is to model the business not some physical computer file structure—Remember, the first logical design principle and the prime directive is separate logical from physical.

Logical data modeling is concerned with attributes that are legitimate business properties of entities. An identifier is an attribute that uniquely determines (points out) an entity or relationship instance. Common identifiers are employee numbers, social security numbers, tax id numbers, etc.

TYPES OF KEYS

There are dozens of keys used to store data in computer storage. Some of the most common are:

Record ID-The physical location of a record occurrence in computer memory.

Storage Key-Any key or data value used to identify the storage location (Record ID) of a record occurrence in computer memory.

Primary Key-A data field used as the principal method for identifying a record occurrence.

Secondary Key-A non-unique data field used to find all record occurrences with a data field that shares the same data value.

Hash Key-A data value applied to or resulting from a hash algorithm (a formula resulting in a number distributed between two numerical end points) to determine a Storage Key.

Search Key-A data field used to find one or more record occurrences.

Sort Key-A data field used to sort a file.

Surrogate Key-An invented or contrived key to provide uniqueness or to save space.

Database Key (Record Key)-A database management system generated data value to identify the physical location (Storage Key) of a record occurrence in a database.

File Key (Record Key)-A file system generated data value to identify the physical location (Storage Key) of a record occurrence in a file.

Foreign Key-In the Relational Model, one or more fields in one table that have the same definition and domain as the primary key in another table. Foreign keys are used for linking related tables together.

Keys are physical data management concepts that are used, in various ways, to point to a record occurrence in a computer file. To fetch or store a specific record occurrence, the file system must know in what type of memory the record is stored (main memory, disk, tape, etc.). For example, if the record is stored on rotating disk, then the file system must know the disk drive type, the drive number, the cylinder number, the track number, the sector number, and finally the displacement from the beginning of the sector. The concatenation of this information forms the record id.

All keys either point to the record id or to another key that, in turn, points to the record id. It is possible for there to be a chain of keys pointing to other keys, until eventually one points to the record id. All of this is interesting and important, but not to logical data modeling, where it is inappropriate and violates the first logical design principle. So why does it keep coming up? Well, you have to look to a competitor of the Entity-Relationship Model.

Relational database management systems have been the most popular database management system for that last 30 years. The relational database management system is based on the Relational Model, a theory of information management going back to 1969. Edgar Codd, the author of the Relational Model[1], believed that his model was not only a foundation for a database management system but also the basis of modeling the business. Put simply, Codd thought that his Relational Model did a better job of modeling an organization than the Entity-Relationship Model. The problem is, the Relational Model deals not with business objects, but with set theory, functional dependencies, foreign keys, and the like.

In the E-R model, a relationship between entities is a business object expressible in a common language, such as English. In the Relational Model, records (called relations or tables) are similar to entities, however there is no object in the Relational Model comparable to an E-R relationship. Rather a relationship, in the Relational Model, is an attribute in one relation that shares a data value of the same domain with an attribute in another relation. Take the simple parent-child relationship of invoice and line item. The E-R model identifies the data object Contains as the relationship between Invoice and Line Item. In the Relational Model, there is no similar data object; rather the record occurrence (called a tuple or row) Line Item includes an attribute (called a foreign key) of the same domain and containing the same data value as the primary key in the Invoice tuple.

Relationships in the Relational Model just require some duplicate data—an attribute, called a foreign key, in the child relation with the same domain and data value as an attribute (called the primary key) in the parent relation.

A further difference between the Entity-Relationship Model and the Relational Model is that in the E-R model, any identifier must have business significance. In the Relational Model, that is not the case. Take the relation Employee containing the attributes EMPLOYEE NUMBER and SOCIAL SECURITY NUMBER. Both attributes are unique, so which should be the primary key? In the Relational Model, unique fields are called candidate keys. One candidate key is selected as the primary key. Which one? It doesn't matter. In the Relational Model, the selection of a primary key from the list of candidate keys is totally arbitrary. In the Entity Relationship Model, there are no arbitrary attributes, entities, or relationships—all must be legitimate business objects.

While the Relational Model is a successful model for a database management system, it is less fruitful when modeling a business. The problem arises when the Entity-Relationship Model is being used to model the business and some team members insist on including keys in the logical data model.

This mash-up of the Entity-Relationship Model with the Relational Model is the cause of some of the confusion about the definition of a logical data model and its placement in the information process. (See the sections *What About...The Other Data Models?* and *Many-to-Many Relationships, et.al* in this chapter.)

WHAT ABOUT...NORMALIZATION?

Back in the good old days, when files were on tape, or worse, stored on punched cards, the number of files a programmer could have open at any one time was limited to the number of hardware devices. If the IT shop had only two tape drives, then the programmer could only have two files open at a time. If the business wanted to store an additional data field, then it would have to fit into one of the existing open files. The result was some strange bedfellows. Customer files would sometimes need to store transaction or product information. Employee records might store time sheet or department information. Take the case of the timesheet file that stores the employee number, the job the employee worked on, the hours he or she put in, and money credited to the employee for those hours (Table 8.1).

Table 8.1 Employee April Timesheets

EMPLOYEE NUMBER	PERIOD	JOB NUMBER	HOURS WORKED	RATE	AMOUNT CREDITED
1265	April	A456	40	$15	$600
1265	April	C345	40	$17	$680
9945	April	A456	30	$16	$480
9945	April	C345	50	$20	$1,000
6736	April	A456	35	$14	$490
6736	April	D985	45	$19	$855
Total			240		$4,105

Data can be pulled from this file to create a report (Table 8.2).

Table 8.2 Job Summary for April

JOB NUMBER	HOURS WORKED	COST
A456	105	$1,570
C345	90	$1,680
D985	45	$855

Now assume that employee 9945 quits and is deleted from the file as in Table 8.3.

Table 8.3 Employee April Timesheets
After Deleting Employee 9945

EMPLOYEE NUMBER	PERIOD	JOB NUMBER	HOURS WORKED	RATE	AMOUNT CREDITED
1265	April	A456	40	$15	$600
1265	April	C345	40	$17	$680
6736	April	A456	35	$14	$490
6736	April	D985	45	$19	$855
Total			160		$2,625

However, deleting employee 9945 also means that the file no longer contains correct information about jobs A456 and C345 (Table 8.4).

Table 8.4 Job Summary for April
After Deleting Employee 9945

JOB NUMBER	HOURS WORKED	COST
A456	75	$1,090
C345	40	$680
D985	45	$855

For example, the actual labor cost for April for job 456 is $1,570; unfortunately, after deleting employee 9945, only $1,090 shows up. This is an example of a deletion anomaly. There can also be insertion and update anomalies. A data integrity problem occurs in a database when an object that is inserted, updated, or deleted causes an unintended change in another object or objects. For example, you cannot add a new project to this database until an employee is assigned to the project. This is an insertion anomaly.

The goal of normalization is to reduce, if not eliminate, anomalies through a mathematical process applied to a physical database design. In this example, normalization dictates the creation of two files, one for timesheets, and one for jobs. In fact, if the timesheet file is fully populated with all required information, then normalization calls for four separate files (employee, employee pay rate, job, and timesheet)—something impossible in a data center with only two tape drives.

How Normalization Works

Normalization is the application of a set of mathematical rules to a database to eliminate or reduce insertion, update, and deletion (IUD) anomalies. It does this by ensuring that all data items are completely dependent on the primary key for their existence and not dependent on any other data item. The various levels of normalization are called normal forms. The higher the level, the more likely potential IUD anomalies are eliminated. The forms are progressive, meaning the model must be in first normal form (1NF) before it can be in second normal form (2NF), which is a prerequisite for the third normal form (3NF), and so on. Normalization is closely tied to the Relational Model. In fact, they were created and first presented together.[2] Although normalization is tied to the Relational Model, it has a much broader use; in fact, with some adjustments, it can be used, and benefit, any database design for any available database management system product, relational or not. Unfortunately, the adjustments can sometimes be confusing and painful to make.

To normalize a model, every record type must have a unique primary key—no exceptions. This is a big deal because most database management systems do not require every record to have a unique key, including many relational database management systems. However, keys, specifically primary keys, are the soul of normalization.

If you want to normalize your database, then you must pretend that your database management system requires primary keys, which means placing keys in all record types. The good news is that you can always remove these keys after normalization.

Implications to Logical Data Modeling

Normalization can and should be applied to all physical database designs. The operative words are *physical database design*, not *logical data model*.

The logical data model models the information an organization uses in the pursuit of its mission. If that information includes attributes that are identifiers—that uniquely determine an entity occurrence—then they should be modeled. However, the data modelers should model only what is there and not invent new data. If there is an identifier for Customer, then it must be modeled; however, if no identifier exists, then the logical data modeler should not create one. Remember: model the organization, not the technology (the first logical design principle: separate logical from physical).

The physical database designer might convert business identifiers into database keys. If a key is required and there is no business identifier, then the physical database designer might create one. However, this is a job for the physical database designer and not a job for the logical data modeler. Because of the key requirement, normalization must wait until physical database design.

Some logical data modelers like to help the physical database designer, and jumpstart the physical design process, by creating identifiers where none exist in the organization. Jumpstarting any task, no matter how well intentioned, leads to errors, missed tasks, and incomplete work. (The perils of this are described below in the section *What About...The Other Data Models?*)The project manager, if not the logical data modeler, must ensure that each logical data modeling task is fully and correctly completed before moving on to physical database design.

WHAT ABOUT...THE OTHER DATA MODELS?

There can be considerable confusion about the term *data model*. Back in your grandfather's day, a data model referred to the type of database management system. The most common types of database management systems were hierarchical, network, inverted, relational, and object-oriented. Today, the term *data architecture* is preferred for referring to the database management system type.

Although most people conflate data model with logical data model they are quite different. A logical data model is a data model much in the same way a poodle is a dog. German shepherds are also dogs and physical data models are also data models.

This does not mean that some other terms aren't bandied about that have identical, similar, or completely different definitions and uses. I look at two, the conceptual data model and a different definition and use for logical data model. I start with the logical data model controversy.

The Hybrid Logical Data Model

Some systems development approaches require that certain normally physical database design tasks be performed during logical data modeling. I have already mentioned the Relational Model and its requirement to assign primary keys to all records (entities). Although most developers see the Relational Model as the theory behind the relational database management system, its author also saw it as a means of documenting the information an organization uses in performing its mission, placing it is competition with the Entity-Relationship Model. The result of this interpretation is a logical data model with primary and foreign keys and without many-to-many relationships, and group and multi-valued attributes, to name a few of its implications. (See the section *What About...Many-to-Many Relationships, et.al* in this chapter.)

The relational logical data model is a hybrid of the Entity-Relationship Model and a database design—a sort of griffin or aberrant logical data model. This approach presents some problems for the project manager and nightmares for the systems development lifecycle manager. However, there is a proposed, though misguided, work-around that uses the conceptual model.

The Conceptual Model

A conceptual data model is, or should be, another name for the logical data model. For many systems developers, however, a conceptual model, or conceptual data model, is a higher-level logical data model incorporating fewer data objects. This conceptual data model is usually reserved for senior business managers who do not need to see all of the detail of the full logical data model. The problem with a level-of-detail distinction is that the distinction is rarely definable. The two models (conceptual and logical data models) are really one model with a different level of detail. It is far wiser, and less confusing, to simply call it that: a logical data model with varying levels of detail—the approach taken in this book. As presented in Chapter 6, the E-R diagram, which supports the full Entity-Relationship Model, is the detailed diagram. A draft or end-user view of the E-R diagram, showing only the most important entities, relationships, and attributes, is called the end-user diagram. The phrase "end-user diagram" better reflects the use of the model without giving it a name that inflates its importance.

Some modelers have a unique use for the conceptual data model. They contrast the conceptual model with the hybrid logical data model required by the Relational Model. For these developers, the conceptual data model is THE abstract representation of the business, while the logical data model—containing keys and eliminating many-to-many relationships, etc.—is the model passed on to the physical database designers.

A Short History of Logical and Physical

The word *logical* in IT means non-physical or abstract. A computer can have one or more physical disk drives that can be configured as any number of logical disk drives. A physical file can be part of a larger logical file or made up of multiple smaller logical files. Link editors convert a computer program's logical memory addresses to physical memory addresses. The same is true for workstations, databases, and many other information technology objects. In IT, *logical* is contrasted with *physical*; where *logical* represents the conceptual or abstract, and *physical* represents real things, such as CPUs, disk drives, and workstations.

The distinction between logical and physical processes goes back centuries, long before the first real computer, when logical process models were used to, among other purposes, conceptualize factory designs, which drove the physical factory floor plans.

The logical model represented *what* the user wants while the physical model represented *how* to deliver what is wanted. The logical *what* and the physical *how* are the cornerstones of delivering functional and efficient systems.

In systems development, the logical model is the abstract representation of *what* the system does or should do, while the physical model shows *how* the physical system does it or should do it. Logical data models model the business not the technology.

The Logical/Physical Distinction in Systems Development

The end-result of systems development is an application consisting of computer programs and a database or one or more data files. Traditionally, building an application follows two separate although interconnected paths: a process path and a data path. The process path starts with a user's view of the processes or functions that are part of the system, followed by a more technical description of those processes and functions, that are input to the programmers who create the computer code that makes up the final application (Figure 8.3).

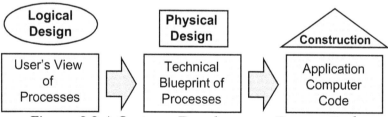

Figure 8.3 A Systems Development Process Path

As pointed out in Chapter 1, the path can be part of a waterfall development approach (where each step is executed, in sequence, once and only once) or an iterative/incremental development approach (where each step is executed, in sequence, as many times as required, with the duration of each step being months, days, or hours).

The data path is similar. The initial phase is the user's view of the organization's data, followed by a technical blueprint of the data that is the input to database schema design (Figure 8.4).

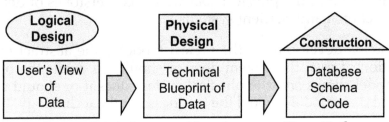

Figure 8.4 A Systems Development Data Path

As different as process and data modeling are, they cannot be performed in isolation. Process modeling uncovers the data that it needs, while data modeling uncovers new uses for processes. They are separate disciplines, but they cannot be performed separately (The Second Logical Design Principle—Distinction). There must be close coordination between the process and data teams. It is like trying to walk with your feet tied together with a one-foot long rope. It doesn't matter which foot you start with; you are not going very far without bringing up the other foot. Do one without the other, and you fall flat on your face. Luckily, the different phases of systems development—logical design, physical design, and construction—are usually performed together with constant team interactions, shared working papers, and jointly developed deliverables feeding nicely into each other (Figure 8.5).

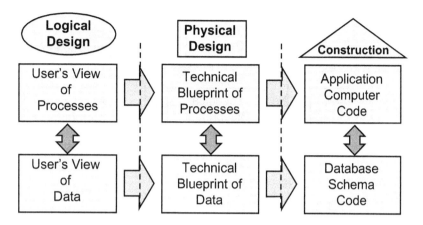

Figure 8.5 The Process and Data Phases Lineup

Why keep logical and physical separate? Simple. The goal of systems development is to build great systems, and painful experience shows that when logical and physical are kept scrupulously separate, better systems result.

However, there is a fly waiting to get into the ointment, and it is the relational hybrid model. In the hybrid approach, the conceptual data model is the logical representation of an organization's or system's data, the physical data model is the physical representation of an organization's data, and in between, in some data no-man's land, is a hybrid logical data model that is part conceptual data model and part physical data model.

What's the Big Deal?

Ideally, as mentioned above, the different modeling phases lineup. There is a logical process modeling phase and its corresponding logical data modeling phase, and there is a physical process modeling phase and its corresponding physical data modeling phase. However, if data modeling produces a hybrid logical-physical data model, then development phase alignment is off because there is no hybrid logical-physical process model, potentially playing havoc with process-data coordination (Figure 8.6).

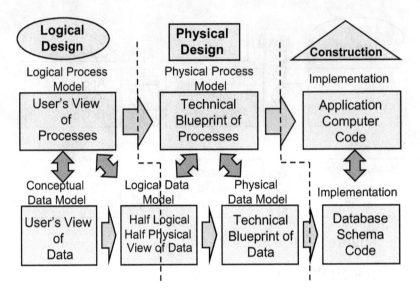

Figure 8.6 Adding a Hybrid Logical Data Model
Disrupts the Process/Data Alignment

The only way modeling—process and data, logical and physical—make sense is if the phases in which the models are developed are aligned, producing models at the same level of abstraction.

What's a Logical Data Modeler to Do?

The first step in solving any problem is to understand the situation. Understanding the situation involves complete and accurate definitions of each term and concept. The definitions lead to the rules and guidelines consistent with systems development goals. Lastly, the rules and guidelines are applied to the specific problem.

This book defines a logical data model as an exclusively abstract representation of the subject's data, sometimes referred to as a conceptual data model. The construction of the model must be consistent with the three logical design principles. Performing these tasks should define, for all, the conceptual data model, the logical data model, and the physical data model and eliminate the problem of the aberrant hybrid logical data model.

WHAT ABOUT...MANY-TO-MANY RELATIONSHIPS, ET AL.?

Want a good test of whether a logical data modeler understands the first logical design principle? Look at an E-R diagram he or she created for many-to-many relationships. Most organizations have a number of them; for some businesses, more than 10 percent of their entities are in at least one M:N relationship. If the diagram you are reading does not have any M:N relationships, then there is a good chance that its logical data modeler does not understand the three logical design principles.

Want to confirm your observation? Look for two entities in a one-to-many relationship with a third entity with a strange entity name such as the concatenation of the two parent entities or containing the word "junction."

Although the M:N relationship is a legitimate end-user concept, some modelers insist on "resolving" them during logical data modeling. The justification for this inappropriate action is usually one of two excuses: conformity to the Relational Model or database management system limitations.

Conformity to the Relational Model

The Relational Model, the theory behind the relational database management system, does not consider a relationship between two entities or records as a data object in the Entity-Relationship sense. Instead, a relationship is defined as the situation where an attribute in one entity or record instance contains a data value of the same domain as an attribute in another entity or record instance. The attribute in the child record, with a data value that is the same as the parent's primary key, is called a foreign key. Relational Model relationships are established using duplicate data. However, the primary key/foreign key scheme can only represent a one-to-many relationship—it cannot represent a many-to-many relationship.

If a logical data modeler is using the Relational Model to build his or her logical data model, then all M:N relationships must be eliminated to conform with this key requirement.

Database Management System Limitations

Most current database management systems support only one-to-many relationships and do not support many-to-many relationships. During database design, the M:N relationships (Figure 8.7a) might have to be *resolved* into two one-to-many relationships with the introduction of a *junction* or *intersection* record or table (Figure 8.7b). Because it must be done eventually, the obvious question to ask is, why not resolve them during logical data modeling? The answer: because a junction record is an artificial construct that hides the end-user fact that a many-to-many relationship exists.

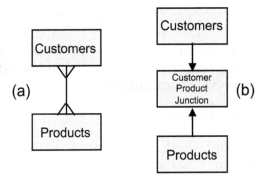

Figure 8.7 (a) A Many-to-Many Relationship,
(b) "Resolved" by a Junction or Intersection Record

Resolving M:N relationships is a database design issue that might (or might not) have to be undertaken during database design. After all, who knows what database management system the database administrators will use or what database management system will be available in 10 years. The logical model should be immune to all physical issues so that the physical designers can separate user requirements from physical design limitations. This is a classic case of legitimate user-related information versus physical design expediency.

There is, however, one case where resolving might incorrectly seem to occur, and that is where the relationship has attributes of its own. Then an associative entity should be created to store attributes about the relationship. For example, an automobile has a list price, but it might sell for a totally different amount. The exact price of a car is dependent on who is buying the car and when (Figure 8.8).

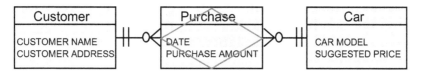

Figure 8.8 An Associative Entity Should Not Be Used
to Resolve a Many-to-Many Relationship

However, an associative entity is not intended to resolve a many-to-many relationship, and it should NEVER be used to covertly resolve such a relationship.

When reviewing a logical data model, the modeler must ensure that the associatives are attributed relationships and not resolved many-to-many relationships. Put as clearly as possible, there are junction records in physical database design; however, there are no junction entities in logical data modeling.

Other Examples of User Requirements Versus Physical Expediency

Most non-relational database management systems support group attributes and multivalued attributes while most relational database managements systems do not. To prepare for physical database design or to make the physical database designers' task easier, some logical data modelers resolve group attributes by either making them a separate entity or simply removing the group and listing the group members separately. Multivalued attributes are shuffled off into a separate entity.

As well intentioned as this resolution might be, it violates the first logical design principle, the separation of logical from physical modeling. If the resolution is required, the physical database designer not the logical data modeler should perform it during physical database design.

WHAT ABOUT...DATA WAREHOUSES AND BIG DATA?

The database management system is essential to transaction processing, the handling and recording of data from single events. Transaction systems are designed to quickly and accurately store small amounts of information, apply transformational algorithms, retrieve and modify on demand, and precisely report on their status. The database management system is the backbone of operational processing.

However, there is a second use for the database management system—providing management and subject experts with the capability to dig deep into the voluminous data created by the operational systems and uncover any trends and patterns they may contain. Unfortunately, the database design required to maximize the efficiency of operational databases is not the optimal database design for management and subject expert queries. A second database customized to this particular processing is required—the *decision support system*. The basic decision support system includes: (1) a user frontend or interface, often containing analytical and mathematical tools; and (2) a storage system or backend to house the data the user interface analyzes.

The decision support storage system, usually a database management system, houses read-only copies of large volumes of historical transactional data. It works this way. Periodically, information from the operational databases is read, the data are often processed, cleansed, or modified in some way and then added to the decision support database. Analysts then peruse the data, looking for useful trends. For example, a supermarket decision support system might look to see which products are bought together or in what quantities. This information can then be used to bundle products or offer coordinated specials or coupons.

Decision support systems have a history going back more than 50 years. Over that time, they have changed and evolved; however, they remain fundamentally the same, although they are often given new names. They have been called a data warehouse, data mart, knowledge base, information base, multidimensional database, data cube, and information repository. The introduction of cheap large-capacity disk drives led to the new moniker, big data.

All of these decision support iterations share the following characteristics of: (1) use copies of operational data, (2) are essentially read-only, (3) are very large, (4) are used, not to look up individual transactions, but rather to synthesize trends, and (5) can sacrifice precision if required.

Although the operational database management system, used for transaction processing, works well as the decision support system repository, the operational database design does not. The need to store and process large amounts of data at a time, with minimal inserts and updates, requires a totally different physical database design. For example, the operational database for an order entry system might include customer and product information, while there might be two different decision support databases, one for customers and a separate one for products.

However, more than just separate databases are required. The physical database design, which does such a good job in processing transactions, is grossly inefficient for a decision support database. New database designs, such as the star schema, are needed. A *star schema* (also called a *snowflake schema*) is a database design with a single *fact record* in the center surrounded by multiple *dimension records* (Figure 8.9).

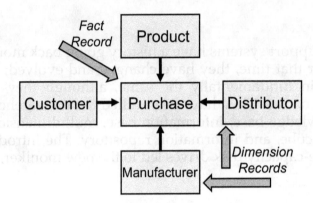

Figure 8.9 Star Schema Showing Fact and Dimension Records

The analyst selects one or more dimension records and then follows them down to the associated fact records.

In truth, before the decision support system is complete, the neat star has often morphed into a more complex structure; however, philosophically, it is still the pristine star.

What does this have to do with logical data modeling? Absolutely nothing! Well almost.

Because the physical database design for a decision support system is so different from the physical database design for an operational system, some systems developers believe that the logical data models should also be different. This is a false conclusion and a big mistake.

Logical data modeling is based on the definition of the data, not on their use. Physical database design—all physical database design, be it for an operational system or for a decision support system—takes the definition of data (from the logical data model), adds to it how the data will be used (from the logical and physical process models), and completes the task by applying environmental constraints (the rules of the database management system being used) to arrive at a database design. The first part of this process, the logical data model, is the same, regardless of the use of the data or how they are stored.[3]

So, when the user, or the physical database designer, or the application programmer asks for a decision support logical data model, hand him or her the same logical data model used for that transaction processing system.

CHAPTER NOTES

[1]Edgar F. Codd, "A Relational Model of Data for Large Shared Data Banks," *Communications of the ACM*, Volume 13, Issue 6, June 1970, pp. 377-387.

[2]Ibid.

[3]George Tillmann, *Usage-Driven Database Design: From Logical Data Modeling through Physical Schema Definition*, Apress, 2017.
Contains information about building a data warehouse from a properly constructed logical data model.

Afterword

Now, there are two different attitudes towards learning from others.
One is the dogmatic attitude of transplanting everything,
whether or not it is suited to our conditions.
This is no good.
The other attitude is to use our heads
and learn those things that suit our conditions,
that is, to absorb whatever experience is useful to us.
That is the attitude we should adopt.
~ Mao Zedong

I like to think of my behavior in the sixties as a "learning experience."
Then again, I like to think of anything stupid I've done as a "learning experience."
It makes me feel less stupid.
~ P. J. O'Rourke

To the Reader,

This book was a group effort. Many logical data modelers, some knowingly and many more unknowingly, contributed to this book, one way or another. Let me explain.

I spent 4 decades of my life working on system development projects primarily in logical data modeling and physical database design. For more than 4 years, I was a member of the ANSI/X3/SPARC Study Group on Data Management Systems, a national organization to study and recommend database management system standards for the IT industry. Years ago, I was one of the designers of a database management system for a computer manufacturer. My consulting career led me to work on dozens of logical data modeling and physical database design projects on five continents. However, like many systems developers, I learned most of what I know not just by doing, but also from watching, and especially by talking to many information management experts about their best and worst experiences.

In my professional travels, I noticed that many logical data modelers struggle with incomplete knowledge, academic gobble-de-gook, and old DBA tales that simply are not true. I have written other books on logical data modeling and database design that focus on helping experienced systems developers trying to build the systems that the textbooks and college classes only talk about. The purpose of this book is a little different. It is to introduce logical data modeling and physical database design to those just starting out, although I include a few tidbits for seasoned modelers as well.

Have I been successful? Well that is where you come in. I am a practitioner and not a researcher. My goal is to share with other professionals what they need to know and what they are likely to encounter in the real world of information management. This is a book for those in the corporate trenches and not the ivory tower. As such, my criteria for success is not approval from academic researchers but from the data modelers working in those corporate trenches.

I am interested in hearing from readers like you about your data modeling experiences—the good, the bad, and the ugly. I would like to know if this book helped you, where I got it right, and where I missed the mark. You can send your stories to me at my email address below. Who knows…maybe there will be another data modeling book sometime in the future with your experiences used to educate the next generation of information experts.

If you like this book, write a review and either send it to me or post it online, such as on Amazon or Google.

You might also be interested in some of my other IT books.

> *A Practical Guide to Logical Data Modeling (Second Edition)*, Stockbridge Press, 2020. Discusses logical data modeling in detail and with practical advice for the working logical data modeler.

Usage-Driven Database Design: From Logical Data Modeling through Physical Schema Definition, Apress (a division of Springer) 2017. Lays out a framework for turning a logical data model into a working physical database design independent of any particular database management system.

Project Management Scholia: Recognizing and Avoiding Project Management's Biggest Mistakes, Stockbridge Press, 2019. Discusses the 17 most serious project management mistakes and what to do about them.

The Business-Oriented CIO: A Guide to Market-Driven Management, John Wiley & Sons, 2008. Discusses the challenges and workable solutions for IT managers and chief information officers.

Best,

George Tillmann
george_tillmann@gmx.com
georgetillmann@optonline.net

Glossary

Abstraction A representation of a subject that excludes unnecessary detail while focusing on important features.

Acceptable Values A list of the only values an attribute can have.

Almost Unique Identifier (1) An attribute type whose data values are rarely duplicated. (2) An attribute that is unique during only part of its life. For example, a business might be able to guarantee that a number is unique only for a certain period of time.

And A logical operator that states that, given the compound statement (A and B), the compound statement is true, if and only if, the simple statement A is true, and the simple statement B is true.

Association The role a subtype plays for its supertype.

Associative Entity A relationship that has its own relationships and/or attributes.

Atomic Attribute see Simple Attribute

Attribute A property of an entity such as COLOR, NAME, EMPLOYMENT DATE, or SOCIAL SECURITY NUMBER.

Attribute Complexity The intricacy of an attribute. There are two types of attribute complexity, simple and group.

Attribute Domain see Domain

Attribute Occurrence see Attribute Value

Attribute Source The origin of an attribute. There are two sources, primitive and derived.

Attribute Type The set of all objects that are a single property of an entity.

Attribute Valuation The number of values an attribute can have at any one time. There are two types of valuation, single valued and multivalued.

Attribute Value An attribute occurrence. A single case of an attribute type.

Attributive Entity An entity whose existence depends on another entity. It is also called a weak entity.

Bachman Diagram see Data Structure Diagram

Basic Physical Data Model The output of Transformation, the first physical database design step.

Best Practices An experienced-based collection of rules, advice, and insight regarding the correct, most effective, and/or productive application of one or more techniques.

Bill of Materials (1) The representation of an n-level hierarchy where n is unknown. For example, a parts model where a part can be composed of other parts. (2) A recursive relationship that represents an n-level hierarchy.

Binary Relationship A relationship between two, and only two, entities.

Cardinality The maximum number of occurrences of one entity type that can be related to the one or more occurrences of another entity type. Cardinality is expressed as one or many.

CASE see Computer-Aided Software Engineering

Clustering Placing one record occurrence on the same database page as another record occurrence so that the physical I/O to access one occurrence will also access the other occurrence.

Combined Usage Map Multiple individual usage maps combined into a single map.

Communication Principle (The Third Logical Design Principle) Clearly deliver information requirements to both users and technical staff in a manner most useful to each. Requirements must be clearly stated and understandable by all audiences and consist of detail that illuminates.

Compound Identifier Two or more attributes used together by the business to identify an entity occurrence.

Computer-Aided Software Engineering (CASE) A software product consisting of a number of different tools that automate parts of systems development. Upper CASE includes automated aids for performing data and process modeling. Lower CASE is concerned with code generators and testing tools. CASE tools that include both upper and lower CASE are sometimes called integrated CASE or ICASE.

Concatenated Identifier see Compound Identifier

Conceptual Data Model see Logical Data Model

Conceptual Model see Logical Data Model

Conjunction A Relationship Constraint in which if an instance of entity A is related to an instance of entity B, then it must also be related to an instance of entity C. For example, if a Customer has a Credit History occurrence, then it must also have a Credit Plan instance. Conjunction is derived from the logical concept *and*.

Construction The third systems development phase that includes coding and testing.

Customization The fourth physical database design step in which the performance of the Functional Database Design (Database Schema) is improved using the advanced features of the file manager or database management system. The result is an Enhanced Database Design (Database Schema).

Data Aggregate see Group Attribute

Data Dictionary A repository of detailed documentation and other useful information about logical and physical data and process objects. The dictionary can be as simple as a loose-leaf binder or as sophisticated as an automated library system.

Data Element A property of a record type such a COLOR or NAME. Also called a field.

Data Flow Diagram A graphical representation of the logical movement of data within an existing or planned system.

Data Item A generic term for a data element, or field.

Data Model (1) A representation, using text and/or graphics, of the definition, characterization, and relationships of data in a given environment. There are two types of data models, logical data models and physical data models; however, when used without the logical or physical modifier, logical data model is assumed. (2) No longer used, the database management system architecture (hierarchical, network, relational, etc.).

Data Model Diagram The graphical representation of data.

Data Modeling Objects The building blocks of a data model. The three basic logical data objects are entities, attributes, and relationships. The three basic physical data objects are records, data items, and links.

Data Modeling The process of identifying and representing the definition, usage, and/or storage of data.

Data Objects see Data Modeling Objects

Data Repository see Data Dictionary

Data Structure Diagram Also called a Bachman Diagram. The first graphical data modeling technique, created by Charles Bachman in 1969, which depicts entities or record types as rectangles and relationships as arrows.

Data Type A programming language term that identifies broad domain categories, such as Integers, Real Numbers, Text, and Currency.

Data Value An attribute occurrence.

Data Warehouse A storage system to support decision support system data.

Database Design Rationale A journal that records the decisions made in the creation of a physical database design.

Database Management System A software system to manage the storage, access, and update of information.

Database Schema The software instructions to create a database.

Database Schema Definition (1) The computer readable instructions for building a database. (2) The output of the Formalization and Customization physical database design steps.

Decision Support System A system that provides management and subject experts with the capability to dig deep into the voluminous data created by the operational systems to uncover the trends and patterns they contain. The basic decision support system includes a user interface, or frontend, often containing analytical and mathematical capabilities; and a storage system, or backend, to house the data the user interface analyzes.

Degree An indicator of the number of entity types that exist in a relationship. There are three types of degree: unary or recursive, binary, and n-ary.

Derived Attribute An attribute that is the result of a calculation or algorithm applied to one or more attributes (primitive or derived). For example, the derived attribute TOTAL AMOUNT is the sum of individual AMOUNT attributes.

Derived Entity (1) A set of entity occurrences that is defined by part of another entity's definition, an inaccurate representation of that definition, or a combination of multiple entity definitions. (2) An entity created specifically to store a derived attribute.

Descriptor Attribute A not necessarily unique characteristic or property of an entity or relationship.

Detailed Diagram (1) An E-R diagram (2) complete logical data model diagram, often application oriented, providing a view of the organization's entities, relationships, and attributes. (3) The logical data model diagram which, along with the data dictionary, is the logical data model.

DFD see Data Flow Diagram

Disjunction see both Exclusion and Inclusion

Distinction Principle (The Second Logical Design Principle) Distinguish logical data modeling from logical process modeling. All data definitions, characteristics, and relationships need to be analyzed, designed, and documented in a manner that captures their relevant information independent of any use.

Domain The set of possible values of an attribute type. There are three types of domains. Data types are broad categories of data values, such as text, integers, and dates. Ranges are values between end points, such as years between 2000 and 2030. Acceptable values are a list of allowed values, as with the values USA, EU, and UK.

DSD see Data Structure Diagram

Duplicate Data Two or more attributes with the same name or definition.

Embedded Attribute An attribute with multiple facts "buried" inside; e.g., ACCOUNT NUMBER might be made up of the data items "branch code" and a "sequence number within branch."

End Users Those who are experts in a system or routinely use the system. They are usually non-technical staff (unless the system is designed to serve technical staff, e.g., an application tracking system).

End-User Diagram A high-level end-user view of the data an organization uses, usually developed during planning or at the very beginning of analysis. It includes only the basic entities and relationships with examples of attributes. End-user diagrams are commonly discarded after project completion.

Enhanced Database Design The output of the Customization physical database design step.

Enterprise Data Model see Enterprise Model

Enterprise Model A model, or series of models, that describe an entire organization or enterprise. There are two enterprise models, an enterprise process model and an enterprise data model.

Entity A person, place, or thing about which an organization wants to save information.

Entity Fragment Diagram A view or portion of the data model that supports a specific process. Entity fragment diagrams are useful for logical process modelers who want to understand the data used by a particular function or to elicit process information from end users.

Entity-Relationship Diagram (E-R diagram) The logical data model diagram created using the Entity-Relationship Model.

Entity-Relationship Model (E-R model) An approach to logical data modeling, introduced by Peter Chen in 1976, that focuses on the non-technical "business" data objects of entities, attributes, and relationships rather than physical or technical objects such as files, records, and databases.

Entity-Relationship Pair A sentence construct (Entity-Relationship-Entity) that represents a binary relationship.

E-R Model see Entity-Relationship Model

E-R Diagram see Entity-Relationship Diagram

Exclusion A Relationship Constraint in which an instance of entity A can be related to an instance of entity B, or to an instance of entity C, but not both. For example, either a Dealer or a Customer can own a Car, but not both. Exclusion is derived from the logical concept of *exclusive or*.

Exclusive Or A logical operator that states that, given the compound statement (A exclusive or B), the compound statement is true, if and only if, the simple statement A is true or the simple statement B is true, but not both.

Extended Entity-Relationship Model A series of extensions to the E-R model to expand its functionality (e.g., supertypes and subtypes).

Facilitated Joint Session A gathering or workshop of a number of users together, along with a data modeler as a facilitator, to build a complete data model. The goal is to have the attendees talking, back and forth, primarily among themselves, with, as needed, help from the facilitator.

Foreign Key In the Relational Model, one or more fields in one table that have the same domain and definition as the primary key in another table. Foreign keys are used for linking related tables together.

Formal Walkthrough A meeting of the users and developers to introduce or reintroduce a model for discussion and acceptance.

Formalization The third physical data database design step where the Rationalized Physical Data Model is modified to reflect the rules and features of the file manager or database management system. The result is the Functional Database Design (Database Schema).

Functional Database Design (Database Schema) The output of the Formalization physical database design step.

Fundamental Entity see Proper Entity

Generalization/Specialization see Subtypes/Supertype

Group Attribute An attribute that contains a fixed number of other attributes. For example, the group attribute CUSTOMER ADDRESS, which contains the five simple attributes CUSTOMER STREET NUMBER, CUSTOMER STREET NAME, CUSTOMER CITY, CUSTOMER STATE/PROVINCE, and CUSTOMER POSTAL CODE.

Hash Algorithm A formula applied to a data item to determine its physical storage location.

Hash Key A data value applied to or resulting from a hash algorithm to determine a Storage Key.

Hashing The application of an algorithm to a data item to derive a physical storage location.

How The technical design for delivering the user requirements. The *how* is contrasted with the *what* that articulates the user requirements.

I/O see Input/Output

Identifier An attribute that uniquely determines an entity or relationship instance, e.g., EMPLOYEE NUMBER can uniquely identify an employee.

Inclusion A Relationship Constraint in which an instance of entity occurrence A can be related to an instance of entity B, or to an instance of entity C, or to both. Inclusion is derived from the logical concept of *inclusive or*.

Inclusive Or A logical operator that states that, given the compound statement (A inclusive or B), the compound statement is true, if and only if, the simple statement A is true or the simple statement B is true, or both are true. *Inclusive or* is often shortened to *or*.

Index A file that stores the value of the search key and the location of each record with that key.

Informal One-On-One Interview A meeting with a single user either to elicit the information about a system in order to construct a model of that system or to verify a model.

Inheritance The transference of the properties of one data object to another data object. For example, in logical data modeling, subtypes inherit attributes and relationships from the supertype.

Input/Output (I/O) Accessing data from (input), or writing data to (output), a secondary storage device, such as a disk or tape.

Instance see Occurrence

Intersection Record see Junction Record

Interview Feedback A meeting to present the results of an interview to the interviewee in order to either gain confirmation or identify and correct errors obtained in the interview.

Isa An invented word to label the association (relationship line) between a supertype and its subtype, so that the reader understands that the association is a role and not a relationship.

Junction Entity The inappropriate and misapplied "resolving" of a many-to-many relationship by inserting, between the two original entities, a third "junction" entity with a many-to-one relationship to each of the original entities.

Junction Record The removal of a many-to-many link between two record types to accommodate database management systems that cannot support them. The database designer creates a junction record type between the two original record types. The single many-to-many link is then replaced with two many-to-one links to each of the original record types.

Key One or more data items used to identify a record occurrence.

Logical Data Model A data model of the information used in an organization from an end-user perspective, without regard to its functional or physical aspects. Although its meaning is more specific than the generic "data model," the two terms are often used interchangeably.

Logical Data Modeling The process of documenting and describing end-user data to end users and system developers alike.

Logical Design The first phase in the systems development lifecycle in which the users' view of the application is documented in terms of *what* the user wants not *how* it will be delivered. The logical design deliverables become the input to the physical design phase.

Logical Design Principles The cornerstones of logical design that should always be scrupulously followed. The three principles—separation, distinction, and communication—form the goals or, more precisely, the reason for logical data modeling. Everything that is done, modeling-wise, should be to support one or more of these three tenets.

Logical I/O A request to access a secondary storage device.

Logical Model A Logical Design deliverable.

Logical Process Model A text and/or graphic representation of the existing or planned functional capabilities of an application.

Logical/Physical Distinction The separation of understanding and documenting *what* the user wants (logical design) from *how* it will be delivered (physical design). In systems development, logical and physical are separated because experience has shown that it results in better outcomes.

Mandatory-Mandatory (M:M) The relationship between two entities A and B in which every occurrence of entity A must be related to an occurrence of entity B, and B must be related to A.

Mandatory-Optional (M:O) The relationship between two entities A and B in which every occurrence of entity A must be related to an occurrence of entity B, but B need not be related to A.

Many-to-Many (M:N) A relationship in which an occurrence of entity A can relate, as a maximum, to many occurrences of B, while an occurrence of B can relate, as a maximum, to many occurrences of A. For example, an uncle can have many nephews, while a nephew can have many uncles.

Many-to-One (M:1) The inverse of a one-to-many relationship.

Membership Class The connectivity characteristic that describes how many of one entity type can relate to another entity type. Cardinality and modality describe a relationship's membership class.

Modality The connectivity characteristic that indicates whether or not an entity occurrence must participate in a relationship. If an occurrence of entity A can relate to zero occurrences of entity B, then the modality is optional—an occurrence of A does not have to relate to an occurrence of B. If an occurrence of entity A must relate to at least one entity occurrence B, then the modality is mandatory—there are no cases where an occurrence of A is not related to an occurrence of B.

Model An abstract representation of a subject that looks and/or behaves like all or part of the original.

Modeling The process of creating the abstract representation of a subject so that it can be studied more cheaply (a scale model of an airplane in a wind tunnel), or at a particular moment in time (weather forecasting), or manipulated, modified, and altered without disrupting the original (economic model).

Multivalued Attribute An attribute that can have multiple values at the same time.

N-ary Relationship A single relationship among three or more entities.

Navigation A network model term to describe the programmer- or end-user-controlled movement within the database.

Neighborhood Diagram A diagram containing a single entity, its relationships, and the entities that are directly connected to those relationships.

Normalization A physical database design technique involving the application of a set of mathematical rules to the physical data model to identify, eliminate, or reduce insertion, update, and deletion anomalies.

Occurrence A particular instance, member, or participant of a type, such as the Bob (the occurrence) of (the type) Employee.

One-to-Many (1:N) The relationship in which one occurrence of entity A can relate, as a maximum, to many occurrences of entity B, but an occurrence of B can relate, as a maximum, to only one occurrence of A. For example, a mother can have many children, but a child can have only one mother.

One-to-One (1:1) The relationship in which an occurrence of entity A can, as a maximum, relate to one and only one occurrence of entity B, and an occurrence of B can relate, as a maximum, to only one occurrence of A. For example, a husband can have only one wife, and a wife only one husband.

Optional-Mandatory (O:M) The relationship between two entities A and B in which an occurrence of entity A need not be related to an occurrence of entity B, but B must be related to A.
Optional-Optional (O:O) The relationship between two entities A and B in which an occurrence of entity A need not be related to an occurrence of entity B, and B need not be related to A.

Optionality see Modality

Organization The entire user community of a business or enterprise. The term refers to all types of organizations regardless of their purpose (commercial enterprise, government agency, not-for-profit organization, etc.).

Participation see Modality

Phantom Entity see Derived Entity

Physical Database Design (1) A data model configured to reflect the usage of data for a particular physical environment. (2) The database management system specifications of what the information base should look like and how it should function. (3) A process for identifying and evaluating tradeoffs and calculating the best solution to balance performance and cost for the current and near-term needs of the end user. (4) The tasks for creating the physical data model and the database schema definition.

Physical Database Designer The individual or individuals responsible for creating the physical data model and the database schema definition.

Physical Data Model (1) A physical representation of the logical data model but modified to include all physical characteristics or properties of the data; how applications will actually use the data. (2) The output of the Transformation and Utilization database design steps.

Physical Data Modeling The process of describing and documenting exactly how the stored data appear and how application programs can access and manipulate them.

Physical Design The second phase in the systems development lifecycle in which the user's view of the application is turned into technical design specifications—*how* the *what* will be delivered.

Physical I/O The actual (physical) accessing of information from a secondary storage device.

Physical Process Model A text and/or graphical representation of a system (hardware and software), focusing on what the system does or how it should perform the functions identified in a logical process model.

Primary Key A field (or multiple fields) that, in physical data modeling, functions as an identifier in a record type and is used as the primary method of physically locating a record for storage or access.

Prime Directive see Separation Principle

Primitive Attribute An attribute that expresses an atomic or non-decomposable fact (value) about the entity, as in COLOR is "blue."

Principles see Logical Design Principles

Process Model A representation, using text and/or graphics, of the definition of processes and procedures in a given environment.

Process Modeling Logical or physical modeling that documents the processes or functions of the organization.

Proper Entity A simple or fundamental entity that can exist independent of other entities or relationships.

Ranges A domain type that indicates the acceptable values between two end points, such as Dates Between 1/1/2010 and 12/31/2050, Nonnegative Values Between 0 and 4.0, and Last Names Beginning A To J.

Rationalized Physical Data Model The output of the Utilization physical database design step.

Real World Corollary An addendum to the Separation Principle that states, (a) A logical design is valid if, and only if, it reflects the real (user) world, and (b) A logical design is invalid if it contains non-real (non-user) world objects or concepts. Invalid objects and concepts include elements belonging in physical design, such as foreign keys, pointers, and disk drives.

Recursive Relationship see Unary Relationship

Relational Database Management System A database management system based on the Relational Model.

Relational Model A database architecture created by Edgar (Ted) Codd in 1969. The model is the first information architecture based on a formal foundation of predicate calculus and set theory.

Relational Theory A popular name for the Relational Model.

Relationship A natural connection between entities.

Relationship Constraint A restriction on how entities can relate to each other. There are three relationship constraints: exclusion, inclusion, and conjunction.

Repeating Group see Multivalued Attribute

Repository see Data Dictionary

Role The different parts subtypes play in a supertype.

Schema A physical machine-readable detailed description of a database.

Semantic Data Model see Extended Entity-Relationship Model

Separation Principle (The First Logical Design Principle) Separate logical design from physical design. A simple concept that states: understand *what* needs to be done before figuring out *how* to do it. It is the fundamental, disciplined, and near-universal formula for all systems development.

Simple Attribute (Atomic Attribute) An attribute that does not contain any other attributes.

Single-Values Attribute An attribute that can have only one value at a time.

Structure Chart A diagrammatic physical process modeling technique that represents the process as an inverted tree. The top of the tree is the root system or program level. Subsequent levels are modules representing greater process granularity. The bottom levels usually represent program modules performing a single task.

Subject Area Diagram A subset of a data model that contains the entities and relationships that share certain common business characteristics, and that facilitates the creation and development of, and communication about, the complete logical data model.

Subtype A role an entity plays. The subtype contains the role-specific attributes and relationships. For example, the supertype Customer might play two roles, Wholesale Customer and Retail Customer. Each subtype (role) inherits from the supertype all of the supertype's attributes and relationships. For example, the subtype Retail Customer can inherit from Customer the attributes CUSTOMER NAME and CUSTOMER ADDRESS. However, each subtype can have its own attributes and relationships. For example, the subtype Retail Customer can include the attribute LOYALTY PROGRAM NUMBER.

Supertype An entity that contains multiple roles that the entity can play. The roles are called subtypes. For example, the supertype Customer might play two roles, Wholesale Customer and Retail Customer. Each subtype (role) inherits from the supertype all of the supertype's attributes and relationships. For example, the subtype Retail Customer can inherit from Customer the attributes CUSTOMER NAME and CUSTOMER ADDRESS. However, each subtype can have its own attributes and relationships. For example, the subtype Retail Customer can include the attribute LOYALTY PROGRAM NUMBER.

Systems Development Lifecycle (SDLC) A formal process for the planning, analyzing, designing, developing, testing, and implementing of a computer-based system.

Technical User Systems developer who uses the output of other system developers. For example, programmers use the programming specifications written by other system designers.

Technique A series of steps applied to a subject to change its representation. Data modeling, processing modeling, and prototyping are all techniques.

Three Logical Design Principles see Logical Design Principles

Tool A physical or conceptual construct that assists in the application of a technique. CASE products and flow-charting templates are tools.

Transformation The first physical database design step in which logical data modeling objects are converted to physical data modeling objects. The result is a Basic Physical Data Model.

Type A class or set of objects that share a distinguishing factor.

Type-Occurrence Distinction (Type-Instance Distinction) The difference between a class of objects, the type, and a particular occurrence or instance of that type. For example, Employee is a type while the particular employee, Bob, is an occurrence or instance of that type.

Unary Relationship (Recursive Relationship) A relationship between two or more occurrences of the same entity type.

Unique Identifier see Identifier

Usage Analysis The understanding of how the database will be used (data creation, access, update, and deletion).

Usage Map (Usage Scenario Diagram) The graphic resulting from applying a usage scenario to the logical data model.

Usage Scenario A step-by-step listing of how a process, uncovered in process modeling, uses the database.

Usage Scenario Diagram see Usage Map

Usage Scenario Map see Usage Map

User A person or persons associated with a system. There are three types of users: end users, user management, and technical users. When used alone end user is assumed.

User Management Those who commission or fund a system or represent those who commission or fund it. They are usually nontechnical staff, unless the system is designed to serve technical staff, e.g., an application tracking system.

Utilization The second physical database design step in which, using the process models, the Basic Physical Data Model is modified (rationalized) to accommodate how the data will be used. The result is a Rationalized Physical Data Model.

Value An instance or occurrence of an attribute type; a characteristic or fact about an entity occurrence.

Walkthrough see Formal Walkthrough

Weak Entity see Attributive Entity

What The articulation (text and graphics) of user requirements. It describes the users' understanding of the data and functionality of an existing system or of what a new system should include. The *what* is contrasted with the *how* that articulates the technical design for the requirements.

INDEX

www.ingramcontent.com/pod-product-compliance
Lightning Source LLC
Chambersburg PA
CBHW060558060326
40690CB00017B/3747